Praise for *Crisis Averted* and Evan Nierman

Evan Nierman's evocative new book Crisis Averted *lifts the curtain on the unseen dramas of crisis management, especially among those with the most to lose.*

—Edwin Black
New York Times *Bestselling Author of* IBM and the Holocaust

With his first book Crisis Averted, *Evan Nierman is stepping into the public sphere and revealing what I have known for years: his understated approach belies a sharp intellect and deep understanding of policy, politics, and people. These qualities, paired with his integrity, have made him a trusted counselor.*

—Ben Carson, MD
Former Cabinet Official, Former Presidential Candidate, Retired Neurosurgeon, and Bestselling Author

Helpful and fascinating, Crisis Averted *is teeming with real-life examples of the best and worst outcomes and provides practical advice for creating your own crisis toolkit. I now understand why being right is not enough; we all need to be prepared.*

—Cynthia Cleveland
YPO International Board Director
YPO International Networks Chair
Former Global President, Universal Studios Consumer Products
President, Imaginarium and Teleflora

In Crisis Averted, *Evan Nierman convincingly portrays a much-needed message for business leaders: better to prepare for a PR crisis beforehand than react to potential PR threats in today's fast-moving world. Having dealt with several PR challenges in previous businesses, as I read his wise words all I could hear myself saying was, "Where was Evan when we needed him?" Well, he's here in* Crisis Averted!

—Jack Daly
CEO Coach and Amazon Bestselling Author

Crisis Averted *by Evan Nierman smartly explores the complex worlds of crisis management and international PR. It's a valuable resource for dealing with the global media from one of the best in the business.*

—Avi Issacharoff
Maariv *and* Times of Israel *Middle East Analyst*
Cocreator of Netflix hit show Fauda

Crisis Averted *shares Evan's vision and is a valuable resource for leaders in pursuit of communications excellence.*

—Professor Yitshak Kreiss, MD, MHA, MPA
Director General of Sheba Medical Center

This book is a real-life look at what it's like on both sides of the crisis matter—client and counselor. There's an old saying in our industry: "Use your peacetime wisely," because in crisis, time is a commodity you just don't have. So use your peacetime wisely and read this book. You will be very glad you did.

—Richard Levick

Chairman and CEO, LEVICK

When it comes to politics and business, one key element that you have to get right is communication. Crisis Averted *is a fresh examination of how to deliver messages that matter in today's information age.*

—Senator Joe Lieberman

Former Vice-Presidential Nominee

Crisis Averted *should be required reading for all successful business owners who want to stay that way!*

—Jason Loeb

Sudsies Founder and CEO
President of EO South Florida

When the stakes are high and your reputation is on the line, Evan Nierman is the guy you want in your corner. For more than a decade, I have trusted him with our firm's clients across a range of industries.

—Bruce March

Greenberg Traurig Shareholder and Cochair of the Firm's Global Corporate Practice

Evan sets himself apart in Washington, because he focuses on long-term success and building strong relationships. Crisis Averted *is a window into the workings of a talented communicator who truly knows how to get things done.*

—Congressman Brian Mast

Crisis Averted *is an invaluable resource for entrepreneurs and executives in every industry. Riveting real-world examples and concrete, no-nonsense guidance for handling the inevitable challenges of business make it a must-read!*

—Mark Moses

Author of International Bestselling Book Make Big Happen
Founding Partner of CEO Coaching International

No book on crisis management and corporate communication comes close. Evan Nierman is a master of his craft, which makes him a vital resource for smart CEOs seeking world-class PR counsel.

—David Samrick

Chairman and CEO of Mill Steel Company

Crisis Averted *is an entertaining and educational book from a truly masterful crisis manager and communicator.*

—Armstrong Williams

Entrepreneur, Author, and National TV Personality

CRISIS AVERTED

CRISIS AVERTED

PR Strategies to Protect Your Reputation and the Bottom Line

EVAN NIERMAN

Advantage.

Published by Advantage, Charleston, South Carolina.
Member of Advantage Media Group.

ADVANTAGE is a registered trademark, and the Advantage colophon is a trademark of Advantage Media Group, Inc.

Printed in the United States of America.

10 9 8 7 6 5 4 3 2 1

ISBN: 978-1-64225-257-6
LCCN: 2020924870

Layout design by Wesley Strickland.

This publication is designed to provide accurate and authoritative information in regard to the subject matter covered. It is sold with the understanding that the publisher is not engaged in rendering legal, accounting, or other professional services. If legal advice or other expert assistance is required, the services of a competent professional person should be sought.

Advantage Media Group is proud to be a part of the Tree Neutral® program. Tree Neutral offsets the number of trees consumed in the production and printing of this book by taking proactive steps such as planting trees in direct proportion to the number of trees used to print books. To learn more about Tree Neutral, please visit **www.treeneutral.com**.

Advantage Media Group is a publisher of business, self-improvement, and professional development books and online learning. We help entrepreneurs, business leaders, and professionals share their Stories, Passion, and Knowledge to help others Learn & Grow. Do you have a manuscript or book idea that you would like us to consider for publishing? Please visit **advantagefamily.com** or call **1.866.775.1696**.

To Robin, Noa, and Gabe, who inspire me every day. I believe in you.

—Evan

CONTENTS

INTRODUCTION:

A CRISIS AVERTED

Allow me to set the scene for you. The CEO was playing fast and loose with the company finances. He set up his mistress in a luxury penthouse. Fancy dinners, extravagant gifts, the whole nine yards. He thought he was being discreet, but someone on the board of directors caught wind of it. A meeting was called, a decision made: swift removal. No second chances.

Lover boy was the face of the firm, and a scandal would send shock waves through the industry. This had to be done on the down low. He had to disappear in short order—jettisoned without a trace of impropriety.

The board confronted him with evidence, advised him to step down, and told him just how it would be done. A press release would paint him in positive but muted terms, and he was not to say a word. There would be a mutual nondisclosure agreement; he would get a severance package and quietly go away. Which is precisely what happened.

It is a classic example of public relations crisis management—or, in this case, a crisis averted. This profession centers upon high-stakes and high-profile situations that are hard to forget but are often best handled quietly without the world ever knowing or truly understanding what took place behind the scenes.

No person or organization is immune from experiencing a crisis. It is not a question of if, but *when*. Before the text messages begin flying and the dominoes start to fall—that is when you need to employ the will and skill to make the right moves at the right time.

You cannot learn this in a textbook. It won't be properly covered in any graduate school curriculum. In fact, I would argue that a measured, academic approach is exactly the wrong way to become an effective crisis counselor. It has to be learned on the job. In real time. And you absolutely have to think on your feet.

In *Crisis Averted* I am going to provide a peek behind the curtain. I will highlight the remarkable power delivered by strategic communications done right, and provide insight into the vital, but little-known and often misunderstood, niche of communications known as crisis PR.

My hope is that sharing my approach and some of my personal experiences will empower you to apply many of these lessons in your own life and in your own business. The goal is to provide you with tools that you can utilize immediately, and to help you develop the mindset and the skillset needed to navigate our hyper-connected and media-driven world.

If the information in *Crisis Averted* helps even a single good person avoid a bad outcome, then it will have been worth the effort.

As you will come to understand, crisis managers are entrusted with the most sensitive professional and personal information imaginable, and confidentiality is essential. With that principle in mind, I will not reveal the names of any clients. But rest assured that every single story in this book is true.

PART I

AN INTRODUCTION TO CRISIS PR

CHAPTER 1

AS BAD AS IT GETS

The phone rings. It's a number I don't recognize. I take the call, and a man says, "Is this Red Banyan?"

"Yes," I reply.

"You guys do crisis PR, right?"

"Yes."

"How quickly can you start?"

I say, "Why don't you tell me what's going on. If we are a good fit for what you need, I can have a contract in your hands in the next ten minutes, and we can begin working for you."

"Okay," he answers. "Here's the situation. I'm the CEO of this company. My COO was just arrested. They led him out of the office in handcuffs. He's an unregistered sex offender. Half of my staff just quit. Some of them are starting to blog about what they saw today in the office. The local media has the story, and they're working on it."

I process this, and say, "Well, how do you know? You haven't talked with any reporters have you?"

"Oh, yeah, I did. I gave them an interview already."

Not the answer I was looking for. "Okay. Are you the only person who spoke with the press?"

"Well, no. My sister also chatted with the reporter. I think she actually talked to him twice."

"Okay, when is the piece supposed to air?"

"They're preparing it for the news tonight at five o'clock."

I glance at my watch—it's two o'clock. The police had just frog-marched a top executive out of the building. Needless to say, this one was about as bad as it gets. Then it got even worse. I ask the CEO, "Did you know that he was a sex offender when you hired him?"

Silence.

Then after a long pause, "Well, I was trying to do a nice thing and give the guy another chance in life."

Welcome to the world of crisis PR. A fascinating and fast-moving place where the circumstances are always less than ideal and successful outcomes are never assured.

But rather than upending your organization, there are critical steps you can take to protect your reputation and revenues. In fact, properly preparing for an inevitable crisis may be the single most important investment a company ever makes.

And when you find yourself in a tough situation, that's when having a good crisis manager—or this book—can help.

PR versus Crisis PR: What's the Difference?

It is important to understand that most PR agencies are not crisis firms. A general PR firm's typical function is to push out information that makes its client look good. And that can be whether the client is selling a product or service or, as in the case of a nonprofit organization, promoting a cause or an agenda. For instance, say an organization is concerned with climate change. They will use PR in order to bring attention to that issue so that their opinions can impact the broader conversation.

The difference between general PR and crisis PR can best be explained by an analogy. Say you are having a heart attack, and you have two options. You can go into a surgical theater and have a cardiac surgeon work on you, or you can take your chances with a general practitioner. Which would you choose?

Or here is another example for those who think they can manage a crisis by themselves. Many of us drive cars every day, and some have been doing so for decades. It is a part of day-to-day life. But are we ready to be a professional race car driver? Have we been forced to handle the unique pressures that come with pushing two hundred miles per hour when the margin for error is zero and the possibility of crashing could mean disaster? That is what takes place during a crisis.

When you are in a crisis, you need a specialist and specific types of expertise. Unfortunately, it is very hard for the average person out there to know the difference between firms that specialize in crisis and those that really do not.

Part of the reason it's hard is because of the firms themselves. Out of a desire to drive business and promote a breadth of services, most PR firms list crisis communications among their core competencies. The problem is, the number of firms who actually focus on that type of work are few and far between, and it can be very confusing for anyone seeking the best possible crisis PR support in a time of need. To the untrained eye, it looks like something that everyone does, when that is simply not the case.

The Making of a Crisis Counselor

The difference between the crisis PR practitioner and someone who does marketing, communications, or media relations boils down to experience, skills, and most importantly, nuance. A top crisis PR person will understand the nuances involved with each business across a wide range of industries.

Your client's success can often hinge upon those subtle distinctions in the way you frame arguments, describe situations, and talk about companies. Mastering nuance reveals you as a true subject-matter expert and can be the key to helping reporters or the public understand the truth and why their previous impression of a situation, person, or company is not accurate.

Not everyone has the temperament to be an effective crisis counselor. Another given of the occupation is that you will be exposed to some nasty predicaments. You simply cannot allow yourself to be intimidated by the circumstances or the people with whom you will be dealing, including reporters themselves.

An often-invoked cliché we have all heard is that someone professes to be "a lover, not a fighter." But when it comes to crisis PR, success often depends upon the crisis manager's willingness to go to war for clients to protect their reputation.

Battling negative perceptions is not for the faint of heart or someone who views the world in black and white terms, as opposed to shades of gray. In other words, when the future of your organization or your reputation hangs in the balance you better find yourself a lover and a fighter: a crisis manager who believes in you, loves uncovering and promoting the truth, and is prepared to fight.

Truth in Fiction

To take a deeper dive into the traits that make a great PR crisis counselor, it might be a good idea to look at how Hollywood has defined the role.

Specifically, let's talk about Winston Wolfe, the "fixer" portrayed by actor Harvey Keitel in Quentin Tarantino's masterful film *Pulp Fiction*. And even though most of what happens in that movie thankfully never occurs in real life, it was dead-on in terms of what makes a good crisis counselor.

To briefly summarize, the movie's two hit men need to clean up an accident involving a dead body in a blood-splattered car, and a crisis manager known as "The Wolf" is called in to assist. And just why is he so effective? I think for a few reasons.

> Typically, crises break at the absolute worst times.

One, because he is reachable. When he's contacted by the gangsters' boss, he is in the midst of a family event. It's clearly an inconvenient time to take a call—after all, he's wearing a tuxedo—but he nevertheless makes himself available.

And that's what often happens when you work in crisis PR. Typically, crises break at the absolute worst times. But you have to be willing to drop everything and just get there. And that is what Mr. Wolfe did.

Another thing the film got right was when Mr. Wolfe stated, "I think fast, I talk fast, and I need you guys to act fast if you want to get out of this." If you cannot think quickly and synthesize a lot of information, distill a problem to its essence, clearly communicate next steps, and take action, then you should not be in crisis PR, where speed is vital.

And here is another strength of "The Wolf." He has the ability to interact effectively with people at the top of society, as well as with thugs. That duality, I believe, is a quality that also serves crisis managers well. They need to be just as comfortable talking with a CEO as with a blue-collar guy working on the production line. When a crisis presents itself, the crisis PR expert needs to be able to speak to people on their terms.

Lastly, you have to be willing to walk away. Mr. Wolfe knows he can fix their problem, but when he encounters resistance, he reminds them that, while he is there to help, if his help is not appreciated, then they can go it alone. And that is sometimes what you have to do as a crisis counselor. If a client won't listen to reason or persists in making poor choices that you believe will cause harm, then you must have the courage to voice your concerns and even give up the account by stepping aside.

So yes, the parallels between Winston Wolfe and a real-life crisis manager are there. But just for the record, I don't know of any crisis managers who have ever had to dispose of a dead body in a junkyard.

Litigation PR—Another Strong Suit

Now let us take a look at the world of general PR versus crisis PR and see if we can break it down even further. Typically, the ultimate measure of success in general PR is how many times you can get your client into the media. Conversely, a crisis PR specialist is often judged by how many times you keep your client *out* of the media.

There is also another branch of public relations to be aware of: litigation PR. Not all crisis PR is litigation PR, but litigation PR does fall under the greater umbrella of crisis PR.

Litigation PR refers specifically to situations where communications counsel is brought in to work on a matter that involves legal issues. It could be defending a lawsuit; in some cases, it involves initiating one. You should always bear in mind that the legal process is one that plays out in a very structured manner and usually over a long timeline.

All you need to do is look at the dockets in different jurisdictions to understand that the legal process, as it currently stands, is broken with little hope of quick repair. Once a suit is filed, it takes a very long time for a case to reach resolution. It is almost always years. Certainly months.

The rub is you have a very slow-moving, almost glacial legal process. And in the meantime, the media is a living, breathing organism moving extremely fast. So, acknowledging the difference between the two, if you have a media or PR strategy that works in tandem with your legal strategy, you can accomplish things outside the courtroom. And in the end, oftentimes it matters less what happens in court than what happens in the court of public opinion.

Litigation PR can be a vital way for a plaintiff to put pressure on a bad actor and to expose them publicly. It's also an option for putting them on notice that they should really settle their case before things get worse for them.

And in other instances, some people use PR as a cudgel. They attack people who have not actually done what they assert in their complaints and smear organizations that don't deserve it. We see it happen all the time. It's executed by unscrupulous PR outfits who understand how to play the game of media manipulation in order to make one party look bad.

Who's Got Your Back?

Bottom line, a top-notch crisis PR firm should be judged not just by the good press stories it secures for its clients, but by its ability to refute and defuse explosive negative stories, sometimes killing them entirely.

When involved in serious and high-stakes matters, it helps immensely if people in the media recognize your crisis PR firm as one that is professional, accurate, and possesses a reputation for integrity and honesty. Given that they are your representative, you should seek out someone who will reflect positively on you or your organization.

If you are a CEO or someone in a C-suite position at your company and do not already have a PR crisis counselor, then you should get one. Seriously. And before the inevitable crisis happens, you should take the time to go through a vetting process so you can be confident in your choice.

During tumultuous times, having confidence in your crisis PR firm is everything, because you have to experience a sense of comfort and feel like whatever happens, there is someone who truly has your back.

Sometimes just knowing you have someone standing beside you when you are at your most vulnerable makes all the difference, especially when that commitment is backed up by experience and competence.

So how do you know when you have a crisis? In the next chapter, we will talk about what a crisis looks like. It often doesn't start out as

CHAPTER 1: AS BAD AS IT GETS

a hair-on-fire event. In fact, if you can spot the signs early enough, you can help prevent that smoldering ember from turning into a five-alarm blaze.

CHAPTER 2

THE MANY SHADES OF CRISIS

A shooting range visitor turns the gun on himself.

A company suffers a massive data breach and has to inform its customers.

A housing facility for elderly patients has a mold outbreak—which is particularly deadly for those with compromised immune systems.

A CEO, arrested years earlier for a personal offense, is the target of a damning article that puts his mugshot on the front page of a top newspaper.

Botched surgeries at a medical clinic leave patients physically disabled for life.

A man and his wife are found dead in an apparent murder-suicide inside a luxury apartment complex.

Fake Google reviews by competitors aim to destroy the reputation of a family-owned business.

There is no getting around it; bad news travels *fast*. Call it human nature, but negative stories are shared far more frequently than good news. The German term *schadenfreude* may have something to do with it. That SAT-worthy word describes a sense of feeling better about yourself when hearing of someone else's misfortune.

> There is no getting around it; bad news travels fast.

There is also that age-old newspaper adage that still holds true in today's media-saturated society: if it bleeds, it leads.

Some of the examples listed at the start of this chapter are literally matters of life and death. Others are not, but they could still prove disastrous to the reputation and livelihood of an individual or business. The point is that there are many different types of crises, coming in various shapes and sizes and levels of intensity.

While similarities abound, each person and organization must contend with a set of circumstances that is unique to them. But there is an important common thread linking many crises: people or organizations are often not attuned to the warning signs of danger ahead. Either they are not looking for them, or the signs simply get misinterpreted.

The most extreme example of this sort occurred at Pearl Harbor in December 1941. A serviceman operating a recently installed radar unit spotted a large incoming blip on the screen he was monitoring. He reported his finding to the officer in charge and was told "not to worry about it," as it was probably a squadron of American bombers returning to the base. History proved otherwise.

The takeaway of this rueful lesson is this: it is often difficult to recognize when an actual crisis, requiring skilled intervention and decisive action, is at play.

Here, we will discuss how a potential crisis can present itself, talk about how such an event can appear to different organizations, and also paint a picture of how hard times are not necessarily hopeless—even sabotage can be salvageable.

Crises Come in All Shapes and Sizes

When it comes to recognizing a crisis, keep in mind that people are seldom the best judges of determining whether or not they are actually in one. This is especially true when a dangerous situation is in its early stages. Skillful crisis management is all about how you perceive the circumstances as they unfold. What one company may believe is a crisis event may be ignored by another that does not see the circumstances in those terms at all.

Even well-informed business leaders often fail to understand that they have a crisis on their hands. Whether this is a result of outright denial, a C-suite leader trying to maintain an optimistic outlook and posture in the face of a challenge, or plain ignorance is no matter, since the outcome can be the same.

The misguided or misinformed may harbor the false belief that existential disasters, sensational headline-grabbing developments, or major meltdowns are the only incidents that require damage control, crisis PR, crisis communications, and crisis management.

They are wrong. Yes, situations involving deaths or injuries certainly qualify as crises. But beyond these extreme examples, companies will often choose to endure what qualifies as a "crisis" even if they do not believe it rises to that level. And that can be a costly mistake.

Every organization that says to itself, "Oh, wow, crisis PR—we would never need that kind of help" or believes "nothing that serious is likely to happen to us," is taking a very shortsighted view. What this hyperconnected digital age shows us all is that even small incidents that appear insignificant can rapidly spiral out of control. Situations do not need to literally be matters of life or death in order to make an impact and carry the threat of mass destruction.

Like Volcanoes, Crises Can Erupt Quickly

For pretty much every organization, the potential for crisis is akin to a volcano. There may be a lot of activity taking place beneath the surface—out of sight—that can rapidly rise and morph into full-scale eruption.

For instance, an employee getting arrested over the weekend—even when it has absolutely nothing to do with the workplace—may produce a full-blown media maelstrom for you and your company. Or think about someone who blogs about a negative experience they had with one of your customer service representatives. Posted on social media, a negative screed can take on a life of its own. Next thing you know, your entire brand is being impugned, and you pay the price as sales plummet.

Reviews Matter and Can Directly Impact Your Bottom Line

As a case in point, there was a memorable situation where a small, family-owned business had flawless Google and Yelp reviews. Not only did those great reviews promote the business, but they were a major point of pride for the owner.

Until he got one bad review from a customer. And while that single negative review certainly did not constitute a crisis, he saw it as one. The fact that this person was hurting his perfect five-star rating on Google drove him crazy. So he ended up calling and threatening the reviewer. Not a good move, and it did not end well. In fact, his failure to act with a cool head and a proportional response ended up multiplying his woes exponentially.

The reviewer then posted the threat he received online and took it to the local news. And before you know it, people came out of the woodwork. They were so offended by the owner's heavy-handed tactics that they started bombing his company with one-star reviews.

Instead of one unfavorable review, which the man incorrectly saw as a crisis, he quickly amassed dozens of negative reviews from people whom he did not even know. And as a result, he actually wound up in crisis and will be dealing with the fallout for some time. Those reviews continue to impact the public perception of him and his company, and they will do so for as long as he stays in business, because some of the reviews and all of the news stories are never going away.

His impulsive and wrongheaded behavior made it hard to credibly defend himself later as a good guy who made a mistake. Instead, the overreaction itself served only to reinforce the perception of the online mob that descended on him: that he was a jackass worthy of scorn.

That one example shows that situations can arise quickly and may not immediately be recognized as a crisis. No, this was not the *Exxon Valdez* disaster, but it shows how missteps, even on a much smaller scale, can have catastrophic outcomes on a business.

The lesson here is that some people may think that crisis PR is an extravagance, something out of their league that they cannot afford.

But nothing could be further from the truth. Crisis PR does not just apply to Hollywood celebrities or multibillion-dollar corporations. It matters for organizations of every shape and size.

In fact, effective crisis management more than pays for itself, because it helps preserve the most precious commodity a company ever possesses—its reputation.

It May Not Be Your Fault

Sometimes, a crisis can erupt even if you have the best of intentions, do all the right things, and no one on your staff is directly responsible. That may be the truth, but that does not mean it will matter one iota. After all, the public typically does not pause to carefully consider the details. People know what they hear and then swiftly draw their own conclusions. That is precisely why skilled crisis management is crucial in the early stages of a developing story. I'll show you what I mean.

One day we received a call from a business located near our Florida office. They were a dance academy that used a transportation service for children enrolled in their classes. A van driver would pick up the children at school and then drive them directly to their after-school dance activities. Of course, the children's parents had given their permission to allow the kids to be shuttled from school directly to the dance studio.

This all went off without a hitch, until the day when one of the children was left in the van. The child had fallen asleep in the back seat, and the driver did not notice her. It gets really hot in south Florida, but thankfully the worst did not come to pass.

Instead, the kid woke up sweaty, looked around, and thought, "Oh, I'm in the van. Where is everybody? I guess they are all inside."

She unfastened her seat belt, stepped out into the sunshine, and walked into the building to join her friends for class. When she came through the door, the dance instructors immediately did the right thing. Concerned that the child might be dehydrated, they sat her down in the air conditioning, put a cool rag on her neck, and gave her lots of water to drink.

They then called the mother and explained what happened. And the mother totally freaked out. She contacted the local news, and the next thing they knew, a sensational story of child neglect and endangerment was about to be splashed all over the airwaves.

It was an accident with no harm done. The child was perfectly fine. Did not matter. The frantic mother pressed charges, and the police arrested the driver. The owners of this small company were themselves traumatized because, all of a sudden, they had local TV crews descending on their studio.

There were reporters in the parking lot ready to take video of children walking in and out of the building. Facebook and other social media lit up with breathless details of a crime scene investigation. Just like that, the developing story created a potentially devastating consequence for this small local business.

In the heat of the moment (pun intended), the dance academy owner was in danger of losing control of the narrative. She needed to communicate openly and transparently with the other parents about what had happened—and about what *didn't* happen. There were procedures in place to make sure the kids were counted when they got on and off the van. It was just that the driver failed to do it. He didn't abide by the rules.

I use this as an example to illustrate that every company will inevitably face a situation where they need help. In this particular case, the dance academy owner and the staff had no idea how to handle the reporters. They didn't know what to say when addressing the media, and on top of that, they felt an escalating fear that they might go out of business because of a single mistake by one contract employee.

The child was not harmed, but the incident could have irreparably damaged their brand or even put them out of business if they had not acted swiftly by calling in our team to contain it.

> Every company will inevitably face a situation where they need help.

The owner and her employees could have become unemployed. And of course, the dozens of kids who looked forward to their dance classes might not have been able to go anymore because the place could have been shut down.

Those were the circumstances when I fielded the panicked incoming phone call. I will take you through a detailed recounting of what happened. The point is not to position myself as some sort of hero or to use this book as a self-promoting marketing piece. Instead, the idea is to give you an unflinching look at the entire blow-by-blow of managing a crisis so that you can draw upon these same techniques should you ever find yourself in a situation with similar challenges.

Rapid Response and Decisive Action

While still on the phone with the panicked owner, I began driving to the studio collecting all the information that I could. By the time I pulled into the parking lot where a news van sat waiting, I already had collected the details and prepared a proper course of action. I went inside and introduced myself to the owner. The fact that I was physically there to assist seemed to calm her down immediately.

And I explained, "This is what we are going to do; this is what you are going to instruct your front desk employee to say and do if the press tries to come inside." I gave her copies of my business card and said, "I'm here now, so send all in-person or other media inquiries to me. If I am not here with you, hand them my card and say 'This is our media representative. This is the only person who can speak on behalf of the business so please contact him.'"

Then I went outdoors and engaged the reporter inside the van. I talked him through what did and did not happen. I provided, very transparently, information that enabled him to be much more measured and less sensational in what ended up being reported that night on the news. By explaining the facts, I was able to make it a far less ominous report because the child was never in danger.

It went from being—in the reporter's head—a dramatic story of a child left for hours in a hot van on the brink of death to a much more matter-of-fact report. Having access to credible information and knowing how to provide it to the reporter in the proper way enabled me to influence the coverage and minimize its impact. In fact, the reporter was sincerely grateful that I helped reframe the situation by providing the facts needed to more accurately report the story.

In addition, I negotiated with the reporter and his TV crew about how they would shoot the scene for their piece. Because I approached the subject in a very respectful way, we connected on a personal level. I said, "I would like to ask that you not film the faces of the children as they are going into the studio. Please take their privacy into account."

I pointed out that we did not actually know which kids were in the van and which were not. The safe assumption was that most of them had nothing to do with the incident and, therefore, should not have their faces plastered on the evening news.

It was a reasonable request, and the reporter agreed to it. I followed up by asking him not to bring the cameras inside the studio. I stressed that it was pointless trying to speak to the owner and staff, as they were not going to grant any interviews, but that I would be happy to give him all the information he needed to do his job. He totally understood where I was coming from, and because I took a respectful and professional approach, he was willing to work with us, thereby lessening the potentially harmful impact of the story.

Next up, I gave the owner very clear instructions about what to say—and what NOT to say—on social media. Having an effective strategy was essential, because she needed the best way to address the parental rumor mill, which was already churning. An untruthful rumor, already spreading like wildfire among the parents, was by far the biggest long-term threat to the school.

The studio owner and I discussed what was at stake. I said, "Look, it is not great for you to have a negative story on television about your business, but the bigger problem is that you have dozens of students who come here every day. And what you don't want and cannot afford is parents withdrawing their kids. If there is a wave of people who start pulling their kids out, then you could literally go out of business in just a couple of days."

It was true; the entire business could be on the verge of falling apart. So, we quickly worked out a multifaceted strategy. In just minutes, our crisis team wrote an email update to all parents, crafted talking points for the staff, and created a social media post from the owner explaining the situation without giving all the details, so as to not open them up to a lawsuit.

Instead, we described the incident within the context of the safety procedures the studio already had in place. We owned up to the mistake, mentioning how the driver was going to be held accountable, and reiterated the care their kids received and that their safety was paramount.

And as it ended up, the dance studio got through the next couple of days and ultimately prevailed. Today, the studio is thriving.

The parents understood. In fact, because the owner communicated key information in a way that was very authentic and transparent, the parents actually rallied behind the place. In effect, their sentiment was, "It is not fair for you to get bad press, since you are caring people doing an incredible job creating a safe and nurturing environment for our kids. This is a truly special, loving place. You do not deserve to be attacked, and we will stand with you."

Because of the way the events were communicated as part of their crisis PR efforts, the dance studio actually created *even more loyalty* among their customers in the wake of what could've been a disaster.

What this story illustrates is that the flip side of every crisis is opportunity. In nearly every instance, a time of crisis can be a gift in disguise because it gives you a chance to rise to the occasion. Crisis situations create chances for your organization to demonstrate, as an organization, who you are, what you stand for, and that you value doing the right thing.

> The flip side of every crisis is opportunity.

Your communication strategy can endear you to your customers on a one-on-one level as well as the public at large. How you handle a crisis can, without question, fundamentally transform the relationship they have with you—often for the better.

Do Something

With the crisis escalating, the dance school owner had the presence of mind to search Google. But many individuals and companies in the midst of a crisis situation don't even have the fortitude to seek help. Instead, they do nothing at all.

With a crisis at the doorstep, they go into panic mode and resort to a tactic I call the turtle, which is just what it sounds like—they stick their heads inside their shells hoping that the bad situation is going to pass. But that is a losing strategy, because a turtle curling up on the highway with a speeding truck bearing down on it is going to get crushed.

Going into turtle mode never works because inaction and indecision will be to your detriment. I am not a fan of the band Rush, but they captured this sentiment in the lyrics of their song "Freewill": "If you choose not to decide, you still have made a choice." When facing the onset of a crisis, you have to do *something*, and working with a knowledgeable crisis manager is very often the best move you can make.

So, how do you know you're in a crisis situation? Is there a good rule of thumb? How would you know if that one negative Google review could potentially sink your business? What would be the tipping point?

If you are not sure, then simply contact a reputable crisis PR firm and ask. In many cases, the situation may not rise to a level where action is actually needed. Sometimes, you just need a dispassionate third party to accurately assess what is going on and provide a reality check, which can also help you avoid making the situation worse.

You should also put aside general notions of what a crisis "is" or "isn't" and consider it in more personal terms. Think of it this way: anything that could potentially make you or your organization look bad, or that is not delivering the message and image that you want, is potentially a crisis for you.

It does not have to escalate into an all-or-nothing matter with bet-the-farm stakes. A crisis can be anything that is going to give people an inaccurate or negative view of you or your company. If that is the situation in which you find yourself, then shed your shell, because it is not going to protect you. Instead, take a positive step toward keeping your reputation intact and discuss your circumstances with a crisis counselor.

CHAPTER 3

PRESS THE TRUTH

In our country, there are many ideals that have shaped our uniquely American character. Taking cues from our forefathers, to be an American is to be brave, rugged, fearless, and independent. Yet among all these admirable traits, telling the truth is held in the highest regard. It is the attribute that is associated with two of our greatest leaders.

There is a story we like to tell about George Washington when, as a boy, he received a hatchet as a birthday present. His father returned home at the end of the day, only to find his beloved cherry tree on the ground. And he called his son over and said, "George, do you know anything about this?" To which little Georgie replied, "Father, I cannot tell a lie; I chopped down the cherry tree."

Of course, that story extolling the virtue of honesty is itself not even true. Never mind that; let's consider another individual, who also sits atop our presidential pantheon. This is a man who held the Union together during the Civil War. He emancipated the slaves, and he was a gifted orator—so much so that students are tortured to this day having to recite his speeches from memory. Still, even though he is remembered for these great achievements, we think of him as Honest Abe. Again, honesty was the quality that defined him. And to be honest is to tell the truth.

Never Tell the Truth

Well, I have to deliver the sad news that we are being misled. No longer should we be telling the truth. In fact, we should *never* tell the truth. Instead, we should press the truth. I will explain what that means in more detail, but first, let me tell you what it does not mean.

I am not advocating lying, telling stories, making things up, or betraying your audiences—quite the contrary. Truth is under assault. More so today than at any time in our lives, or perhaps in our entire history.

Misinformation has been disseminated from sources that would have been unthinkable just a few short years ago. And being subjected to this pervasive misinformation stream, as we all are, only serves to underscore the importance of making sure that lies do not become a part of our day-to-day reality. Instead, now more than ever, we must be diligent in doing all we can to see that the truth prevails.

The fields that are the focus of this book are public relations and crisis management. And in case you have not noticed, PR people sometimes have a bit of a dodgy reputation. They are often described as hacks, flacks, or spin doctors.

These pejorative terms are meant to suggest that we dance around the truth, which in my experience is not the case at all. The approach outlined in this book is diametrically opposed, focused upon helping clients by empowering them to fight for the truth.

In fact, organizations looking to spread their messages and individuals facing crises both share an overriding need to employ accurate information and commit themselves to advocacy and action. As Benjamin Franklin once said, "It takes many good deeds to build a reputation, and only one bad one to lose it." The brand equity that your organization has built up, based on your good actions, can vanish in a moment if you make bad decisions—or if you lie.

And for that reason, honesty truly is the best policy. It is a time-honored maxim that should be taken seriously in the service of an ultimate mission to fight for the truth or, to say it even more forcefully, to press the truth.

Own Your Situation

Now I will give you an example of what it means—the difference between telling the truth and pressing the truth. Telling the truth—the old way—is defensive, passive, weak, and slow.

Pressing the truth, on the other hand, is proactive, assertive—aggressive even. It is fast, confident, and strong. Pressing the truth versus telling the truth is the difference between hoping that your message gets out there one day—and making sure that it does.

It is also the difference between reacting, waiting to see what other people are saying about you and then trying to set the record straight, versus seizing the initiative.

To illustrate the distinction between telling the truth and pressing it, I will tell you a quick story involving one of our clients.

There was a situation involving an individual working in finance who was shamefully discriminated against by his employer. He was harassed at work and ultimately pushed out of his job. He was denied earnings that were rightfully due to him from deals he originated and shepherded to a successful close.

Faced with various forms of overt and subtle abuse from his coworkers and betrayed by his company, he finally appealed directly to the CEO of the private equity firm.

During an in-person meeting in the CEO's spacious office overlooking the New York skyline, he said, "This isn't right. You guys treated me differently, discriminated against me, and are withholding from me bonuses and pay that I rightfully earned. Yet through it all, I have remained a great employee for the firm, and my work produced enormous profits for the business. I am not asking for special treatment—only that you do the right thing."

The CEO appeared to be listening intently. With his face cradled in his palm, his eyes looked upward and off into the distance. After an uncomfortable silent pause that lasted about twenty seconds but felt more like twenty minutes, he took a deep breath, looked the young man straight in the eye, and said, "Too bad for you, and goodbye."

Action Speaks Louder

Now, the employee who was being screwed over could have adopted the passive approach prescribed by the old PR model. Had he opted to simply tell the truth, then he could have just waited for his day in court. And he likely would have waited months, or even years, in hopes the truth would ultimately come out.

Instead, he decided to look for an alternate approach that included pressing the truth.

On his behalf, the members of my team made a few phone calls to a handful of carefully selected reporters. We let them know what happened to this person, how he'd been discriminated against. And it wasn't long before the reporters called the CEO of the company for comment on the situation.

When the CEO realized that his company's reputation was about to be destroyed and that people all over the world were about to see what had taken place there, he thought twice about it. He finally made the right decision. He paid the man what he was owed and allowed him to go on with his life.

That story illustrates what it means to press the truth, not just stating the facts, but putting the full weight of influence behind a message. And as in this example, sometimes just knowing that you are not going to back down is all that you need for a situation to be properly resolved.

The term *press the truth* also refers to the other meaning of the word *press*, as in news organizations. It covers the entire Fourth Estate—the print, broadcast, radio and online media outlets that report on the people, places, and events of the day.

Relationships with the press, cultivated carefully and rooted in integrity, are instrumental to achieving the PR outcomes that organizations desire. Want to make sure that your story gets told? Begin the hard work today of building your reputation as an unassailable source of trustworthy information.

And when reporters do not have to think twice about the messages you deliver, because they know them to be factually accurate and see that you are making their lives easier, then they are more likely to take interest in the stories you send their way.

Adopting transparent business practices and being honest and upfront builds trust with the media, in time helping you compile an enviable network of reporters upon whom you can call. Being on a first-name basis with literally hundreds of media professionals is an asset. Creating true connections through honesty and integrity means that reporters will not only take your calls but also be willing to work with you. That's how to put the power of the press to work for you.

Time Waits for No One—and Neither Does the Media

Before the advent of the twenty-four-hour news cycle, it used to be that you had the luxury of time to tell your story. And at companies that retain only legal counsel to address a crisis, as opposed to legal and PR counsel together, you might hear something like this from the attorneys: "The facts will eventually come out," or "Just be patient; we will have our day in court."

But this era of constant breaking news is totally at odds with that kind of traditional legal advice. That's because in their profession, lawyers are conditioned to operate out of fear. Nine times out of ten, their job is to mitigate risk, which essentially means they get paid to look at a situation with the most pessimistic viewpoint possible. Their primary objective is to reduce the likelihood that clients could be sued, or otherwise legally exposed, so they approach each case from a very defensive posture. And all too often, their advice is to "wait it out."

> In the real-time crucible of crisis management, erring on the side of caution can actually prove to be a fatal error.

Often, a law firm will advise its client to "do nothing at the present time." Their counsel usually stems from a place of good intentions and reflects the correct desire to ensure that nothing is said by the client or the PR team that could compromise the legal efforts.

In some instances, the lawyers place gag orders on the PR team when organizations are under fire, encouraging patience. However, organizations unable to adequately defend themselves by pressing the truth can instead face the very real prospect that by the time they finally get to trial, they might already be out of business.

In the real-time crucible of crisis management, erring on the side of caution can actually prove to be a fatal error. "We don't want to reveal our hand, and we need to wait," is often the precursor to disaster. Many lawyers frighten clients and warn against them defending themselves in the court of public opinion. They say things such as, "If we say anything, then we are going to open ourselves up," or "whatever we say or do could end up being used against us at trial."

While the lawyers have a valid point, this strategy is often doomed to fail. Which is precisely why organizations need assistance from crisis managers with experience handling these types of matters. They can provide crisis and litigation PR expertise that works in tandem with the lawyers.

If companies take their advice exclusively from the legal side and choose to just ride it all out while burying their heads in the sand or taking the turtle approach, then they may not even make it to the end of a trial, which is often literally years down the road.

Done right, skillful litigation PR need not jeopardize anything. In fact, in many instances you are actually strengthening the lawyers' case because you and the lawyers are both advocating for the client, just with different but complementary approaches.

In reality, there is almost always something in the PR realm that can be done on a client's behalf during a crisis. The instances where you absolutely cannot say anything are pretty much nonexistent. The knee-jerk response from many lawyers is, "Don't talk to the media at all, and if they do call you, then just say 'no comment' and hang up."

And that is absolutely horrible advice. Only a lawyer who fails to understand the modern media landscape, and that the old rules no longer apply, would recommend that type of defeatist tactic.

> **Perception is reality.**

The problem with waiting and simply telling the truth as opposed to *pressing the truth* is that in the meantime, perceptions take hold. And perceptions become reality. This is something that cannot be stressed enough: perception is reality. Nobody walks around with a fact sheet about themselves. Rather, it is how you're *perceived* that determines the impression you make with a whole range of people all over the world.

You cannot sit on the sidelines and watch. Now, more than ever, you have to get in the game. After all, time waits for no one, and neither does the press.

The Power of Authenticity

Think about it: there are only a finite number of people with whom you are ever going to physically come into contact in your lifetime. However, in the age of the internet, you can interact with millions, tens of millions, or even billions of people online. So again, this new reality calls out to you and says, "What is the decision you are going to make? Are you going to merely tell the truth? Or are you going to press the truth?"

You have to be an advocate for yourself and your organization. If you are not willing to do that, then other people are going to do it for you. And the odds are, the way that they talk about or describe you won't be how you see yourself or would prefer to have yourself portrayed.

It all boils down to this: Are you going to influence the way that the world sees you, or are you going to simply wait to be defined? And that brings up the next question: How can you get better at owning your personal narrative? Well, part of it is the message itself. Obviously, what you say makes a huge difference, but arguably even more important is *how you say it.*

When you are conveying any message about yourself, the key is to be authentic. That is the secret to why "influencers" have tens of millions of online followers. Whether or not it's true, they are perceived as being real and authentic.

In a sense, we are all marketing experts. Every one of us has been subjected to countless advertising messages all day, every day since birth. And what that has done for us is to fine-tune our sensitivity. If something fails to come across as genuine, then we dismiss it. We can spot a phony a mile away.

And some companies out there are thinking, *Well, people are casting stones at us online. They are saying things that are not true, but we are not going to dignify them with a response.* That reflects the old way of thinking. And it is a very dangerous path to tread. Whether you are a start-up or a large corporation, you simply cannot afford to do that anymore.

Seize Control of the Narrative

Organizations that are wrestling with how to react when a reporter shows interest in them should remember this: If you are not willing to stand up for the facts, then no one else is ever going to stand up for you. And nobody outside your organization even knows the facts as well as you do.

When an outside source writes about a company, whether it be a journalist, blogger, online reviewer, or anyone else, they are interpreting the information that they have gathered through the filter of their perceptions. But if you are on the inside, you know the truth and are uniquely positioned to correct any inaccuracies.

You have to be committed to the concept of pressing the truth, especially in a time of crisis. If you concede your role, then other people who are misinformed, uninformed, or simply making stuff up will do it for you. It all comes down to this: *define yourself before somebody else does.*

As we all know, nature abhors a vacuum, so you better come out and say something on your behalf, because that space is going to be filled. And when you opt out of engaging, then you allow that space to be filled by people who don't have all the facts. Instead, people who don't know you, or anything about you, are the ones shaping how the world sees you.

Turn on the TV at any given time, and you will see people who are being paid to give opinions—on everything under the sun. Whatever the producer of the show decides is the topic, the guests and the pundits will weigh in without thinking twice. If they are paid to talk about something, then they will.

The problem is, if they don't know the people or fully understand the content they are discussing, all they are doing is giving their opinion. And in all likelihood, that opinion is largely bereft of truth or fact. So, in order to press the truth, you have to be willing to engage. You have to be an advocate for yourself.

If you've got a developing crisis, an unfortunate fact pattern, or there are things that have happened for which you want to apologize, then it is much better to tell it yourself, tell it first, and tell it all.

That is how you press the truth. Because if you don't tell it yourself, other people who don't have all the facts are going to be talking about your situation and you will be ceding your authority to them. If you have information that absolves you or explains what happened and provides justification, you need to put it out there. That way, it is far more likely to have a greater net impact.

When you drive the narrative and tell your story, whether it is good or bad, you are the one delivering the information to the public. It gives the impression that you are dealing with the circumstances honestly and openly, and it makes you a credible source.

If there is a story being told that pertains to you and you know the truth about it, then you need to seize the initiative and add your voice to the public discourse. Otherwise, you are counting on others. And if you don't have a crisis manager in your corner, you are basically sending up a hope and a prayer that someone else is going to correctly represent you.

Speak Up on Your Own Behalf

One of the biggest mistakes that people make in a time of crisis is getting caught up in a condition known as "analysis paralysis." By that I mean they are getting advice from all these different people in their lives: lawyers, family members, and friends.

Often, a person in crisis genuinely does not know the best next step to take, so he or she does nothing. They may be trying to think through a cost-benefit analysis of what they could say or do, and meanwhile they don't say anything at all. The story—many times controversial or focused on shocking details—just sits front and center in the media and is rehashed over and over, because no new information is being introduced.

When that happens, all the negative statements and flawed perceptions just cycle through the newsfeed again and again.

Taking an active role in telling your story can be scary, but it can also be exhilarating and liberating. On a personal level, it allows you to explore opportunities that you have to bring positivity into the world. It empowers you to be authentic, to be real, and to speak to the people who've had the biggest impact on your life and let them know what they have done for you and how much you appreciate it.

Living in today's hyperconnected age requires us to be honest with ourselves. Are we going to leave it to chance for others to define us? Or are we going to do the hard work of being engaged and actively shape our own destiny?

The world is watching, but it won't wait long for an answer.

CHAPTER 4

KEEPING A LID ON CHAOS

We all know the two certainties in this world are death and taxes. To which I would add a third: at some point in your life, or in the life of your company, you are going to face a crisis. The facts can vary, and they all won't have the same financial repercussions, but a moment will arise when every crisis is the same.

It is that moment when every person and organization must decide what to do next in order to best protect their image and reputation. You may think you're informed enough to make that call on your own. And you may very well get lucky and be able to weather a crisis situation without ever seeking outside help. But are you prepared to put all that risk on your shoulders, especially when you don't have to do so?

The job of a PR crisis management firm—its main purpose—is to take on that risk and fight for the clients, not only during a time of crisis, but through the aftermath. That's when the hard work is done to restore an individual's or company's good name. The crisis firm's job, too, is to prepare businesses for the inevitable *before it takes place*, so when the day comes that a crisis boils over, they will already have a contingency plan and know exactly what to do.

Experience is the critical factor. When a crisis hits you, it will likely be the first time you have encountered anything that could have such life-changing consequences. But an experienced firm will have worked through similar situations, with nearly identical cause and effect patterns, literally hundreds of times.

Yes, every situation is different; each is unique. But the longer the firm has focused on crisis PR, the higher the likelihood that the overall scenario is similar to something they have previously handled.

Crisis managers rapidly take into consideration many factors and should be able to evaluate a situation and say with a high degree of certainty, whether or not it will escalate and become a full-blown crisis, versus something likely to blow over. That is one of the main reasons it helps to rely on the input and the guidance of a crisis counselor.

The Crisis Response Approach

Once a crisis management agency receives a call, the team immediately assesses the key elements of the crisis through the lens of what they have already encountered. They then develop a threat matrix unique to the event, mapping it against what is hot in the news at the time. This is done to determine whether the crisis situation ties into a major focus of the media at that given moment.

At this early stage, all questions are relevant. How localized is the story, and how will it play in the press? Next, who are the players? Who is the main focus of the story? Is the company in crisis a start-up that people have probably never heard of, or is it a very well-known, reputable organization? Because if they are the latter, there is a higher likelihood that people will be interested in news related to them—especially if it is sensational or negative.

The crisis manager also needs to understand the extent of how public facing the organization is. Are they likely to be of interest to consumers of local media? If the incident is obscure, or the company does not typically disclose their activities or promote their services, then it is highly probable that nobody is going to care. If that is the case, then the local news outlets may not invest their resources in reporting the story, because no one will pay attention.

In a time of crisis, one essential element that is often overlooked is the need for an internal communication strategy. This applies to businesses ranging from small mom-and-pop bakeries to multibillion-dollar corporations. You have to think through who your target audiences are, both externally and internally, and determine the best ways to relate to them.

You also need a messaging hierarchy—and clear designation of who is speaking on behalf of your company. That includes having a press protocol for handling incoming emails or phone calls and knowing precisely what to do should the media show up in person.

Many organizations have neither in place when a crisis erupts, which means their crisis PR team must develop the communication strategy and messaging hierarchy in real time. While experience may enable them to do so effectively, it is far more advisable to think through these steps in advance. Preparation is the best way to prevent a crisis from

> Preparation is the best way to prevent a crisis from raging out of control.

raging out of control. And crisis *prevention* is a service recommended for everyone.

No One Wants to Hear Yesterday's News

The other key variable in a crisis situation is timeliness. Are we talking about something from the past that has already been reported on to some extent? Or something fresh and exciting that is happening now and has not been covered? If it is old news, then you can oftentimes convince reporters to simply move on because there is no juice to the story, no news hook. No news organization wants to report on a situation that has gone stale.

Conversely, if something is connected to a theme that is currently receiving media attention, that is a different story. In recent years, the #MeToo movement has shone a very bright light on abuse of power and sexual impropriety, especially in the workplace.

For that reason, any story that deals with issues regarding sexual misconduct is likely to get more traction in that media environment than it might have three or four years before, when there was less of a focus on the topic. When people have a reference point, issues are more likely to escalate into ones of significant concern.

Then there is the flip side. If there are stories in the news that are a huge focal point and sucking the oxygen out of the room, you can often use this to your advantage. Reporters can often be dissuaded from chasing negative stories on certain topics provided they are so far afield from the news that everyone is following.

I have seen this happen many times when clients had bad news that they had hoped to keep under wraps but were forced to disclose. And then, like a godsend, a negative bombshell broke in the press that had nothing to do with the client's situation. When that happens, a window of opportunity opens and organizations can push out their information at a time when no one is paying any attention, because the public is fixated on the distraction.

In these instances, less relevant stories can benefit from going unnoticed for just long enough to become old news. Then, when the dominant story moves on, no reporters are willing to pick up the thread since it happened in the past and is no longer relevant.

So, yes, sometimes you can catch a break. Because timing is everything, an alert crisis manager hyper-attuned to what is going on in the press can help you use a media distraction to your own advantage.

Be Prepared or Be Sorry

A crisis can rear its head at any given moment. In fact, it will. For every single business, with no exceptions. And the more prepared you are to face it when the time comes, the better off you will be. Here is a first-hand example which I hope you will find instructive.

I share this story not to pat myself on the back for a job well done, but to provide you with a real-world illustration of how all the elements of crisis management need to come into play when a threat to your livelihood is imminent.

Like all food-service establishments, a popular family-owned restaurant was subject to periodic health inspections. During one particular visit, it was determined that the restaurant failed in a couple of categories. It wasn't egregious. There was evidence of the presence of insects, some improperly cleaned grease traps—things that could easily be corrected and were certainly not worthy of shutting the place down. Still, the inspectors had to file a public report on what they saw.

It happened to be a slow week for the local TV affiliate, which was known for running sensationalized news features. Always on the lookout for a juicy story, the investigative team found one when they got hold of the restaurant's health inspection report. Next thing you know, the station ran a "Dirty Dining" segment, and they zeroed in on this one restaurant.

The TV reporter alluded to the most atrocious details saying, "The report found the presence of rodent droppings and live insects on the premises. This could prove evidence of a large-scale infestation." That did it. In the name of crusading journalism, the restaurant was branded as a haven for "rats and roaches."

At that point, the owner knew he had a crisis on his hands. We took his call and started working for him right away. Now I should mention this restaurant was located in southern Florida on the waterfront. It was the rainy season, and at that time of year, roaches always seek someplace dry. Built right on the water in their habitat, it was as if the restaurant flashed a welcome sign to all the native bugs. It was a recurring issue, and the employees had to stay on top of it.

Reviewing the situation, I told the owner, "You need to be prepared because this guy may show up with a camera crew. He might do a follow-up at your restaurant and try to interview you." But the owner thought otherwise, saying, "C'mon, that'll never happen." Again, I told him, "I've seen it plenty of times; you need to be ready. Here's what you need to do."

And we put a plan in place that empowered him to press the truth. We assembled it in hardly any time because we had done it so often for other companies. Our experience gave us an established foundation to work from.

In this case, we first needed a game plan for how to handle the visual side of things, especially the camera. Second, we needed our messaging locked down so that the owner and his employees would know exactly what to say to customers and anyone who asked. Third, we needed a designated spokesperson properly coached and equipped to deliver our core messages.

We also needed a plan for how we were going to disseminate positive information. On top of that, we prepared online and social media components so that we could address questions or comments on the restaurant's Facebook page, as well as people talking about them on other sites, especially Yelp and Tripadvisor, where negative reviews could seriously harm the business.

All of that fell on the external communication side of things. But we also needed a strategy for internal communication. The other restaurant workers had to be told, "This is happening, and here is what you should say if anyone asks." Think about it; every single person who worked there was, in effect, a brand ambassador or spokesperson.

So, say Bob is a line cook in the restaurant and his family or friends see the story about rats and roaches. "Hey Bob, isn't that where you work? Is it really so filthy and terrible?" In response, Bob needs to be ready to say, "This one inspection made things sound much worse than they are. Here are the facts: We knew that we would see an uptick in pests because it is the rainy season. The owner had actually asked the pest control company to come in every day due to the wet weather and was trying to get ahead of the situation. It just so happened that the health inspectors came in and filed their report at that very moment." All the employees were advised to communicate that message.

As I told the owner, "You may get a camera crew walking into the restaurant. You have to know what to do when a reporter starts asking the diners, 'Sir, how was your meal tonight? Are you aware this place was shut down recently by health inspectors?' Believe me, it happens sometimes, and you have to be ready for it."

Everyone understood and we put the plan in action. All the people who worked in the "front of the house," the hostess and waitstaff, knew what to say. They had a script written for them. If a TV crew entered with cameras, they would say very calmly and politely, "Excuse me, we would appreciate it if you do not film here. We are happy to have our press representative provide you all the information you would like, but please stop filming and don't disturb the diners."

That was it. And they were instructed to say it again and again—and nothing else. "Do not react," we told them. "Do not look panicked or create a dramatic scene that could play well on TV." And sure enough, even though I engaged with the reporter and provided him with information, that did not cut it for him. He knew the informative statement would not make for "good TV."

So instead, he showed up at the restaurant after staking out the premises and ambushed the owner. With the camera rolling, the reporter ran up to the owner in the parking lot as he was getting out of his truck. Thankfully, the owner had been prepped by us, so he was able to provide a couple of quick sound bites. He gave the TV crew what they needed to run their segment on the news.

Even though he was nervous, he did not look flustered, because we had anticipated the encounter and rehearsed the scenario. And while he did not care for what was happening, he was articulate, stayed on point, and delivered a calm message that pressed the truth.

While the TV station did run a negative story, which was not the ideal outcome, it was counterbalanced by the owner's quotes.

The story was also tempered by additional comments I gave to the reporter in a prepared statement. So that filled up airtime in the piece as well. And because we kept the cameras out, there were no negative visuals to make the piece eye-catching. Then a couple of days later, according to the schedule we mapped out, we had a plan to shut down comments to deal with social media blowback, but there was almost none of any consequence.

With everyone knowing their roles and pitching in, we had done it. Everybody moved on, and today the restaurant is doing just fine. But if a single employee had not stuck to the plan, a much bigger story would have emerged, and it could have closed their doors for good. As it turned out, the coverage had no lasting impact on the business whatsoever.

The point of this example is that preparation is vitally important. Knowing in advance what to do when a crisis strikes puts you in a favorable and powerful position. Those companies who have methodically thought through the different aspects of what could go wrong with their business have a running start over the ones who only retain crisis counsel when the situation is desperate.

Moving On from Mistakes

Here's a news flash: we are all human, which means we all make mistakes. But that also means there is always a chance for redemption. But what happens when you have to work with a flawed character, someone who has made some serious errors in judgment in the past and needs to move on from them? How do you change the narrative?

Well, these days one very effective way to change perceptions for the better is social media. Social media affords you the opportunity to curate your own messaging and create your own content. In other words, you can control what people see. It provides a unique venue with which to counter existing public perceptions of you.

If all that is out there is negative, or what has recently been said about you is disparaging, then you can use the most powerful arrow in social media's quiver, and that is imagery. Rather than trying to convince everybody that you're a different person from what they've heard, you can actually *show* them. Posting videos or photos that paint a person in a very different light from how they have been judged in the past can dramatically change prevailing attitudes.

> Social media affords you the opportunity to curate your own messaging and create your own content.

For instance, we had a client who was portrayed in media stories as an absolutely horrible individual. He had done something terrible in his youth. Unquestionably, he was guilty, but the incident happened more than a decade before. And since then, he had been a model citizen. A family man. A good father. He had been philanthropic. To the best of his ability, he had made amends.

When we decided to help him, we felt that he should not have to wear a scarlet letter for his entire life based on a youthful transgression, however unacceptable. And so, part of our recommended strategy for him was that he needed to own the past and be accountable for what he did. Rather than attempt to conceal it or pretend like it never happened, we advised him to explain his actions and shift the emphasis from who he was then to the better person he is now.

The imagery he disseminated online showed him with his wife and kids doing charitable activities. That way people could see that he was not the monster that the decades-old news reports made him out to be. Instead of only telling, he gave people a window into who he was and his many positive contributions, inviting them to weigh the entirety of his track record. In essence, when you engage in resetting the public's perception of a person or an organization, a certain metaphor applies—changing the viewpoint from a portrait to a landscape.

Shifting the Perspective to Your Advantage

Think of it this way: during a time of crisis, you are seeing a portrait of a person. You are zoomed in, as if looking through a magnifying lens, able to pick up every imperfection and scrutinize every detail. That is what it is like for someone in the midst of a media maelstrom. And one of the key things crisis managers do is to broaden the picture, so the public doesn't continue their fixation on that one person or the bad decisions he or she has made.

Instead, you want people to understand the landscape, to see the context and complexities of any situation. This can be very difficult to accomplish depending on the media. For example, TV poses a great challenge because it emphasizes short bursts of information. Bullet points and sound bites don't lend themselves to going deep or letting you explain all the circumstances in order to paint a fuller picture.

That is why during a crisis, it is imperative to engage with reporters and attempt to help them grasp the entire scope. You need them to conclude that there is more at play than what is obvious. It is a hard thing to do, because reporters do not have a lot of time. News outlets are increasingly understaffed and their journalists overworked. Anything that you can do to make their job easier while they are working to report a story gives you a chance to help shape the outcome, ideally to your advantage.

Meanwhile, the internet has no time constraints. What is posted online lives on. Tapping into the power of online content enables you to reframe messages that can point the way forward for a person's career or help a company write its next chapter. After a crisis, a critical element is working to redefine online who you are and what the public sees.

People are complicated, and there are many facets to our lives. Every single one of us has done things about which we should be proud. And everybody who has ever walked this planet has also done things they regret.

While you cannot go back in time and erase your mistakes, you *can* make a genuine effort to improve your situation moving forward.

PART II

BAD THINGS HAPPEN TO EVERYONE

CHAPTER 5

NEVER GIVE UP

The New York Times is known all the world over as the newspaper of record. Essentially its reputation means that, in addition to its massive circulation, its news-gathering functions are considered authoritative and above reproach. Or, another way to put it, is that the stories and articles found under its famous masthead are recognized as being thoroughly researched and fact-checked before they ever find their way into print.

Even in this skeptical day and age, when cries of "fake news" erupt whenever someone receives unfavorable coverage, the *Times* is generally regarded as a definitive news source and a standard bearer for responsible journalism.

So, when this particular paper fixes its gaze on a subject, and one of its reporters is preparing a story that will cast an indelible viewpoint regarding an individual or an enterprise, it is not to be taken lightly. Whether in newsprint or digital format, it is assured that a huge number of people will read it or hear of it, and nine times out of ten, they will assume the story is factually accurate.

It was under these circumstances that a school and its faculty found themselves under scrutiny from one of the world's most powerful news organizations. In the works was a story claiming that unqualified instructors were teaching kids with learning disabilities. The pending article had the potential to severely damage the reputation of this well-known, highly regarded private institution.

In the Crosshairs

The school got wind of this soon-to-be-published article, knew what dire consequences it could produce, and considered its options. The very next call was to our office, and here is what I heard from their chief administrator:

"We are extremely concerned. We have had inquiries from the *New York Times.* Many of our parents and financial supporters read that paper, and we cannot afford to be the target of high-profile criticism. We don't really know what the reporter's talking about, but it seems like it's going to be very negative."

The school had received an email from the reporter and shared it with me. It didn't mince words. And sure enough, the tone of the email was aggressive. In it the reporter said she had sent an initial email, didn't get an immediate response, and now issued an ultimatum: "I am proceeding with my story. I have given you fair opportunity to comment, but my deadline is coming up. The story is going forward no matter what, so you can either choose to say something or not; either way my story's moving ahead."

On the Case

That was the situation when the school contacted me. "Okay," I told them, "I am your representative and spokesman. And I am the only person who talks to this reporter until we find out what's going on."

I picked up the phone and tapped in the reporter's number. As many reporters do, she answered in a brusque manner, basically saying in no uncertain terms, "What do you want?" I answered, "I'm calling on behalf of the school. I understand you have some questions."

To which she replied, "I don't really have questions. I am pretty sure of the direction my piece will be heading. I'm just offering you the chance to provide a comment."

In response I said, "Well, okay, why don't you tell me the story as you see it, because I want to make sure that the facts are right." She then told me she had obtained information that the school had unqualified teachers. She said that while the school promotes itself as having an excellent program, the kids who needed the most help, those with disabilities and learning challenges, were not getting the education the parents believed they were paying for. And the reason was that the school employed teachers with subpar credentials.

As the school's advocate, I countered, "That sounds completely false. I don't believe that's the case at all. What I can do is assure you that I will run down all the details and get back to you fast."

Upon hearing this, at first, she was very resistant. "Listen, I don't have time to play your games. My piece is going to print. I just need you to add a comment." I shot back, "No, I'm not going to just give you a quote so you can check that box that says you reached out to the focus of your story." I then added, "You're in a position where you are potentially reporting things that are completely fallacious, and I am not providing a quote until we first determine the facts. At the moment, I believe the entire premise of your story is deeply flawed and 100 percent inaccurate."

I also reassured her, "I'm going to get to the bottom of this, and I'll be your conduit for information about the school. I'm going to work with you and get you information that is 100 percent correct. So, give me a little time and know that I'm on it." Before wrapping up, I pumped the reporter for any information I could get to understand where this story originated. And it became very evident that the parent of a former student had contacted her and been her original source.

Working with the school, I was able to ascertain the likely student in question. We were then able to map out her entire academic history: When did she start? Who were her teachers? I double-checked the academic credentials of the instructors, and it turned out they were all currently licensed and had the requisite training to work with kids who presented her type of learning and behavioral issues. In short, everything the reporter was being told was untrue, and we had the evidence to prove it.

> The first person to provide information has the advantage of framing the narrative.

I called the reporter back and walked her through what I found out. I said, "Look, in the fourth grade, the student had this teacher, and these are her qualifications. She has a master's degree in this area," and so on. Still, the reporter remained highly skeptical. She was holding on to the original allegations and seemingly resistant to accepting the truth that I continued to press.

Why? Because the parent had gotten to her first. And as often happens in the world of crisis PR, the first person to provide information has the advantage of framing the narrative. I was trying to undo a false picture that had already been painted, and that is almost always harder to do than simply starting with a blank canvas.

Fight with Facts

The reporter and I had a series of very heated back-and-forth conversations. It was always professional, but contentious and marked by fierce debate and spirited argument. I continued to strenuously object to some of the things she was preparing to report. She, on the other hand, was convinced I was calling to simply schmooze her and talk her out of doing the article entirely.

Starting with the first phone call, she did not initially rate me as having high credibility. Someone who does not want to be persuaded is not going to allow herself to be charmed. And unfortunately, many reporters view PR professionals as obstacles to the truth, as opposed to facilitators. So again, I started out with two strikes against me, and she wasn't about to budge.

I pressed on by saying, "You have to consider your source: a disgruntled parent whose child wasn't a good fit for the school and ended up not staying there. The mother has an agenda, and she is taking it out on the school. That's why she is saying these things, and they are demonstrably false, which I have proven to you."

We had reached an impasse, and the story was still moving forward, even though I provided the requisite quotes and primary documentation, such as university transcripts to directly refute all false allegations. In a last-ditch effort, I even appealed to her editor, and reporters never like that. Once you go over their heads, which they see as tantamount to tattling on them to their boss, then you can pretty much count on that person never liking you or wanting to collaborate in a cordial manner.

The result—an article focusing on the school containing some false and negative assertions—seemed inevitable. I began preparing the school for the piece to come out, knowing full well that it was likely to be a "he said, she said" with the parent saying one thing, the school challenging her assertions, and the reader left to decide. It was not the best scenario, but after hours of work and hard-fought verbal combat to convince the reporter that she was being led by the nose, we had done what we could.

Then we caught a break that changed everything. Right before the article was to be published, the parent posted on social media: "I can't wait to see how the administrators at (X school) will react when they get ripped in the *New York Times* this weekend."

Incredible. While enraging because it confirmed what I had been saying all along about the source's bad intentions and motivations for making false accusations, it was the best thing that could happen. I promptly took screenshots and sent them to the reporter and her editor. My email said, "I provided you with thorough documentation showing that everything this person has told you is not true. I have also made the case to you that this person has an ax to grind."

I then followed up by saying, "I would like you to see the attached social media post, which the parent put out today. It speaks for itself, and I don't think that the *Times* wants to be in the business of allowing a venerated newspaper to be misled and misused as a tool to advance someone's vindictive agenda. If you have any doubts this is happening, then all you have to do is see for yourself how the parent is crowing about using your paper and its credibility to slam the school, even though what she is saying is not true."

And guess what happened? They killed the piece.

A generalized story ended up running a couple of weeks later, but the newspaper completely removed all references to the school.

There was no mention to be found. The reporter and editor never responded to me with any sort of mea culpa, probably because they didn't want to make it look like I had persuaded them to back off. But the result was exactly what we wanted.

The lesson here is to never give in. Never acquiesce. Especially when you know you are right. If the school had not engaged a crisis PR expert at the sign of a negative story appearing, then they would have been at the mercy of the leading newspaper in the world.

They would have had their reputation sullied. And you could bet that all the parents in the community would have known about it. Terrible press like that could have easily wreaked havoc on their enrollment efforts, and the aftershocks would have lingered online for years to come. Whether what they write is true or not makes little difference. Once the *New York Times* casts you as a culprit and tarnishes your good standing, it can take years to recover, if you can recover at all.

Instead, the school and its faculty stood up for themselves and dodged a bullet.

This whole episode reminds me of a cartoon I once came across as a teenager. My father had it printed out and affixed to the wall of his office with a piece of Scotch tape. It showed a frog lodged in the throat of a heron, ready to be swallowed whole. And he would have been, except that the frog had reached one hand out the beak and was clenching the base of the bird's neck, preventing that final gulp. The caption simply said, "Never give up."

Be Prepared

I have given you several instances of crisis management conducted in real time, as events unfold. But if companies and organizations are willing to invest a little bit on the front end in order to prepare in advance, then it ends up typically saving them a lot of money.

In the example I just gave, could a crisis PR firm have anticipated exactly what the details would be? No, but gaming out the potential threats to the school's reputation in advance would have put us in a much better position when the actual crisis flared up.

> A skilled crisis management team can predict with a high degree of certainty what kind of issues you are most likely to face.

Let's say the school had enlisted a crisis agency to perform a public relations contingency plan for them in advance of any investigation by the media or another controversy. As part of the crisis audit, one of the topics that almost certainly would have been raised would have been allegations against teachers, as well as disparagement of the institution on social media or in the press.

What makes an upfront exercise so important is that on many occasions, crises don't simply appear from out of the blue. It is not as if an organization is just sailing along smoothly and then struck by the hammer of the gods. Almost always, a skilled crisis management team can predict with a high degree of certainty what kind of issues you are most likely to face. More often than not, there is some type of antecedent or clue that your crisis manager would detect as a possible red flag.

Of course, you can't expect to know every detail in advance. No one can prognosticate the future that way. But an astute crisis expert will know the types, especially depending on the industry. For example, if the client is a construction company, then you would think through scenarios such as labor disputes or issues involving illegal labor practices or unlicensed migrant workers.

Your crisis management team assembling a plan in advance would account for the possibility of a building or structure collapsing and injuring or killing people. You would sketch out circumstances involving workers injured on the job and subsequently accusing the company of having unsafe business practices or lax safety standards. Every industry has potential situations that are unique to them, and smart crisis managers can anticipate what they are.

A good way to think about engaging with a crisis manager to help you run through all these scenarios is that you are essentially purchasing media and reputation insurance. I am speaking figuratively, because you cannot literally guarantee that the PR team will be able to fully control what's in the media. Reporters will always have free will and their own editorial process.

But you can be prepared to react and make an already mapped-out decision without panic or hesitation during a developing crisis. And that is an absolutely crucial skill set to have when time is of the essence. In a time of crisis, you cannot rely on guesswork if you want to make sound strategic moves.

And there is an additional benefit to running a crisis audit during a time when you are not facing an impending threat: it's good for you and your company's long-term well-being. If you sat down with a crisis manager and prepared for every glass-half-empty scenario that could disrupt your business, it would reveal weaknesses but could also expose the glass-half-full opportunities that could move your business forward.

The Proactive Nature of a Crisis Plan

It is possible to get ahead of crises. Not all the time, mind you, but if you plan for the inevitable beforehand, it always ends up costing a lot less in terms of money, time, and reputation. The key is, you cannot allow human nature to take over and stifle the smart decision to do advance planning. Too often, organizations of every size display a tendency to put off preparation by saying, "Why should I pay to prevent something that may never even happen?"

Then the manure hits the fan. And because organizations will do anything to remedy a crisis situation once they are engulfed in it, they end up paying crisis PR rates, which are significantly more expensive than what it costs to retain your average PR firm. The reason is you're paying for a specialized service when the stakes are at their highest.

> Being embroiled in an actual crisis is the absolute worst time to be creating your strategy.

When you make decisions during a time of crisis, there is a far greater likelihood that you will make even more mistakes and thereby compound your troubles. Bad decisions often multiply when high-stakes situations present themselves, whether in the headline-grabbing realm of politics, in the mahogany-lined boardrooms of multinational corporations, within small family businesses, or in our personal lives.

That is because people too often take a reactionary approach, responding to events as they occur, with no framework for their decision-making. You are much better off planning and gaming out your strategy in advance rather than when your judgment is compromised by the necessity of doing something, *anything*, to get yourself out of a jam.

Being embroiled in an actual crisis is the absolute worst time to be creating your strategy. In an ideal world, you should map your crisis strategy well ahead of unforeseen circumstances. That is a simple, yet very hard concept for companies to grasp. Because it is a preventive measure, often they don't want to spend their resources on it, even though it's an investment that pays itself off exponentially.

For example, let's say you spend $5,000 doing a crisis audit during a time of operational stability. Just for the peace of mind alone, you benefit from knowing that your crisis game plan has been developed to suit your unique company profile, with what-if scenarios considered, addressed, and accounted for by an experienced professional.

Whereas, if you engage a crisis firm as a last resort or only when you are already experiencing serious problems, the investment goes way up. Just to get started, it's likely going to cost many times more than an audit would.

Everyone has heard the expression "an ounce of prevention is worth a pound of cure." That goes double for crisis management. The irony is that it is both much cheaper and more beneficial to engage a crisis firm beforehand, when they can potentially help you avoid a catastrophe entirely. That is when you gain tremendous value from them.

Conversely, if you wait until a situation becomes untenable, the crisis management firm will require you to spend infinitely more money helping you address or recover from it, when an earlier call to the experts could have prevented the problem in the first place.

Where there is even just a wisp of smoke, a fire is always a possibility. While it may not be immediate, it is seldom a matter of *if*, it's most often a matter of *when*.

When smart organizations realize they are due to experience some exposure or fallout in the press, they typically reach out to their attorneys, with smart ones concurrently putting in a call to a crisis management firm.

Then, while the lawyers prepare a legal strategy, the crisis manager gives the company guidance on how to protect the organization, get ahead of potential bad press, and limit the negative exposure coming their way. And the only way for an engagement to work to maximum effectiveness is to ensure that there is trust between the parties.

Clients need to know beyond a shadow of doubt that whatever they say to their crisis manager will be held in complete confidence. Making that confidentiality known upfront is crucial, because clients must feel comfortable enough to speak with honesty and candor and not withhold information.

A Matter of Trust

I will speak only in generalities here, because I do not want to betray the confidence of my client. But I do want to discuss some of the circumstances behind one company's decision to retain crisis management services, since it carries key lessons that can help other organizations.

In this specific case, the business made some mistakes and received some bad press, and a federal regulatory agency came after them with a vengeance. The government had put out a press release about the company including serious allegations that hurt their business and besmirched their reputation. The company had worked hard to convince their partners and customers not to leave them, that the whole situation was just a misunderstanding. In time, it blew over.

Or so they thought. During my first conversation by phone with the company's CEO, he admitted they had recently dodged a bullet, weathering the initial crisis on their own. "Unfortunately," he said, "we are under government investigation again, and they have found some problems."

With their attorney present, the company met with the authorities in good faith. But it quickly became clear that intimidation was the order of the day and that they were going to need crisis PR support alongside legal representation.

After just five minutes discussing the circumstances leading up to the meeting, one of the representatives from the attorney general's office abruptly halted the conversation, dropped a sheet of paper onto the Formica conference table, and said, "Why don't you have a look at the press release we are going to issue tomorrow if we are unable to reach a suitable understanding today."

The person then walked out of the room, leaving the attorney and CEO to read an explosive draft release filled with dire accusations that would undoubtedly make waves in the press. It's a time-tested intimidation tactic that we have seen on many occasions when companies come under scrutiny by the office of the attorney general.

The AG's office will either imply or pledge to send out a press release. Often, they just come right out and do so as a way to threaten and apply pressure. No one wants to have bad news come out, and when the source of the information is a government agency—whether at the federal or state level—it's instantly viewed by the public as credible.

Many people don't know that the government uses PR tactics as levers to further their own agenda; but they actually do it all the time, in all fifty states. On the one hand, if they call attention to a bad company committing crimes, that's great; it's a means of warning the public. But the problem is that they sometimes do the same thing to good companies, too, and individuals who don't deserve it. In those cases, people run the risk of being unfairly singled out and branded as crooks by a government entity wielding critical media coverage as a weapon.

So, in my consultation with this particular CEO, I spoke bluntly. "Everything we're going to talk about is confidential. People trust us with their deepest, darkest secrets. I just need you to be honest with me, since I will always be honest with you. Our most powerful weapon is the truth."

It is an important message that needs to be understood by those in leadership. After all, they bear responsibility not just for their staff, but for their family members as well, who rely upon their employees to provide for them.

> Our most powerful weapon is the truth.

Moreover, enduring a crisis is a deeply personal experience. Whether or not you actually founded and built the organization, you, by accepting leadership, have chosen to make it a central focus of your career and life. To be attacked, especially by those who possess no real appreciation for the blood, sweat, and tears you have poured into the enterprise, can rock you to the core and compound a swirling tempest of emotions that sometimes cycle wildly between shock, anger, sadness, resignation, dejection, and fury.

When assisting clients, crisis managers should be sensitive to those emotional impacts stirred by crisis and ensure that the person or organization under fire understands that the PR team members will do their utmost to help steer them through it. Forming that client connection is not just important, it's often vital for achieving success.

It can be overwhelming and exhausting to feel like the media is treating you unfairly and public opinion is stacked against you. At such a time, the crisis manager must lay out the pros and cons associated with various courses of action to ensure the best possible outcome.

Often, there is no easy path to restoring a company's reputation. The hours are long, the stakes are high, the pressure is intense, and the work is challenging. The crisis manager must deliver results for the client while simultaneously exhibiting courage and conviction and never giving up when it comes time to press the truth.

CHAPTER 6

THE COURT OF PUBLIC OPINION

Although there are distinct differences between the two, the legal profession and the world of public relations do have something in common: both have been unfairly maligned in the eyes of many. We have all heard the epithets: sleazy lawyers, ambulance chasers, PR flacks, spin doctors—and the list goes on. And it's not hard to figure out where this animosity originates.

Both attorneys and public relations professionals are well-versed in the art of persuasion. Their mastery of language and argument is viewed as somehow unscrupulous, often by people who themselves don't possess those skills in abundance. But when the world turns against you, there is no one better to have in your corner. And when necessity calls for these two professions to join forces, they can give you the fighting chance you need to survive and ultimately prevail.

Alliances are struck with law firms because expertise as a crisis manager often dovetails seamlessly with legal counsel. Instead of being overly possessive about attorney-client relationships, smart lawyers bring in communications counselors, knowing full well that it can help give their clients the best opportunity to win.

Forcing the Issue

To illustrate this concept, I once found myself sitting with a prospective client who had us meet with his attorneys at a well-known law firm in Washington, D.C. The reason he called the meeting between his legal and PR counsel was because he had information about illegal practices by a healthcare company and was considering suing them.

We knew that they were guilty. In fact, they were guilty as hell. We had loads of documentation to prove it in court, and the client wanted them held accountable. And in order to do that, there had been talk of exposing the company's bad behavior in the public realm, thereby incentivizing them to move along more quickly toward a settlement. Both the client and his legal counsel agreed that this was the preferred course of action, rather than taking it all the way to trial and racking up staggering litigation costs.

The Power of PR

This approach brings up an aspect of crisis communication that people don't often consider. When thinking about crisis PR, everyone reflexively draws the conclusion that the primary purpose of a crisis counselor is damage control and defending those who have allegedly done bad things. But in the case just described, the work was being done not on behalf of the defendants, but for the plaintiffs. The aim was to bring attention to bear on bad actors, as opposed to defending them.

The role of the communications practitioner was to go after a company for its illegal behavior and expose them publicly, which would be very uncomfortable for them. What we prepared to do was call into question their values, trustworthiness, and character, which are essential to the reputation of a healthcare company.

We as crisis managers can be instrumental in helping our client's legal team expedite the legal process. Backed by the threat of exposure, the lawyers can then force the issue with the offending company, which is often much more inclined to settle quickly, saying, "You know what? Let's cut our losses and just make this go away before it causes us more pain."

> We as crisis managers can be instrumental in helping our client's legal team expedite the legal process.

The leaders of the healthcare company knew their best outcome hinged on keeping the public from knowing the details so they wouldn't be publicly humiliated and criticized for what they did. And they realized the best approach for keeping things under wraps and minimizing negative publicity was to settle the issue expeditiously, before it became a hot topic in the press.

Our role in this case was to impose the threat of exposing the company's malfeasance. And we made certain they knew that it was not just an empty threat. As a practical matter, we were retained not directly by the actual client but rather through their law firm. That's because it is the lawyer's obligation to do all he can to advance the best interests of his client, and he knows just how effective a weapon crisis counsel can be in their arsenal.

In this case, the ultimate aim was to put an end to the illegal behavior that almost certainly led to the deaths of innocents. People died because of the actions of the healthcare company, which we were prepared to show.

The bottom line is that having a media or PR strategy that works in tandem with your legal strategy can empower you to achieve significant results inside and outside the courtroom. And in the end, the final outcome in court often matters less than what happens in the court of public opinion.

The Firefighter

When faced with incendiary legal matters involving clients, one of the more unique traits of Red Banyan and a select group of other firms is that we don't always serve as the firefighter; often we play the role of arsonist. To explain what I mean, I will serve up real-life examples of each.

First, here is a classic example of firefighting. A client retained us because a disgruntled former employee filed a frivolous lawsuit against them and alleged the firm engaged in the most objectionable behavior one can imagine. It was nothing but lies; none of it was substantiated. Every word a complete fabrication.

But the employee hired a PR guy who knew that he could put whatever he wanted into a complaint—and then issue a press release quoting from that complaint. As long as you operate in that manner, it essentially gives you a way to amplify your allegations, *even if they have no basis in fact.* In other words, you can basically say whatever you want in a lawsuit and then use the media to disseminate those lies. And unscrupulous PR people often do just that.

In this case, our client was being accused of threatening the employee with a weapon that was purportedly in his office, saying things like, "If you mess with me, I'm going to f-ing end you." This employee also accused our client of having various adulterous relationships with coworkers. But it was all false—pure slander.

Meanwhile, the PR guy with zero credibility was making things worse. He did not hesitate to drop misleading press releases, and soon everyone who searched for company news online was instead treated to lurid details of a manufactured scandal. This damaging press coverage ran completely counter to the company's brand, and that's what prompted a call to Red Banyan.

Without a moment to lose, the company's legal team retained us to push back on those allegations. On the fly, we crafted messaging for their stakeholders so they would understand that these claims were patently false. The board members also had to be convinced that the truth would prevail.

Next, we had to contain these online attacks from an SEO—search engine optimization—perspective. Pumping out a steady stream of our own press releases utilizing the right search terms and keywords did the trick. Then reporters began calling, because they were being approached and spun up by the other side's PR team. In short order, we had to set the record straight and get these stories killed before our client became the unwanted recipient of terrible coverage without one iota of truth.

I wanted to make sure that we countered aggressively and that our client was not coerced into a settlement. That was obviously the accuser's intent—using PR to spew lies and pressure the organization to pay her a lot of money she did not deserve.

Ultimately, her scheme failed completely because we defended our client's good name with a public relations effort that exceeded her own. Their PR firm was selling lies, and we were pressing the truth. It was a nasty battle waged in the public arena, but our client fought fire with fire.

Our effort prevailed; they were never able to show any evidence that what they were alleging actually took place. We convinced every single reporter who inquired about this topic not to write the story since the allegations were designed to smear our client and publicly embarrass the organization. The lawsuit ended up being dropped, but our work still wasn't done. In the aftermath, we had to engage in online reputation repair.

Remember, the accuser was using press releases as a way to smear our client, meaning that this false narrative would live forever online. So we drafted our own press releases in order to counter their claims and set the record straight. Then we had to make sure our press releases appeared online, ranking at least as high, if not higher, than the ones from the other side. Which we did. End of story. Victory for the good guys.

The Arsonist and the Power of PR

In instances when crisis managers are called upon to play the role of arsonist, they must be just as aggressive at pressing the truth.

In one particular situation, a legal firm contacted us about an individual who had a pristine reputation, although the attorney knew otherwise. Everywhere you looked—online, in the papers, and across broadcast media—you saw nothing but glowing coverage of this guy.

On TV, he was feted as a prodigy and rock-star CEO, profiled by numerous national news programs. The laudatory coverage of him never seemed to end. He was like a self-perpetuating positive publicity machine.

But his empire was a house of cards. The lawyer who retained us said, "I have all these victims who've been bilked out of their money. This guy is running a Ponzi scheme, and he is hiding in plain sight."

We ended up working with the law firm and, over time, exposed this character and revealed him to be the fraudster he was. Through our contacts, we alerted the media as to his true colors, and it was our work together that did the job. The media that was once his cover ended up being vital in terms of actually getting justice.

The Securities and Exchange Commission wasn't doing anything. Ditto for the attorney general and other agencies. The feds didn't even have him on their radar. The guy had stolen tens of millions of dollars from his victims. And then disappeared.

But we made his crimes big news, in a way that could not be ignored. Ultimately, thanks to the excessive media coverage around this criminal, we received a credible tip as to his whereabouts. At the very time, the media had been calling law enforcement asking why this guy was still walking the streets. Their response was, "We can't arrest him because we don't even know where he is. He's in hiding."

Well, thanks to the national news coverage that appeared, someone dropped a dime on him.

After finding out where he was, we called a key contact in the press and within hours a TV crew was on the ground. They staked out this con artist and then confronted him in a man-on-the-street style interview. The reporter and crew also attempted to interview his wife, who literally ran down a back alley to get away from them. The journalists captured it all on camera.

The story aired nationally. Within days he was under arrest. He pleaded guilty and was sent to prison for nearly two decades. The victims of his crimes finally got the justice that he had previously managed to avoid. That's the power of PR.

Another Type of Legal Hurdle

Even in this enlightened age, many attorneys still refrain from talking to the media in any way, shape, or form during the run-up to a trial or throughout the actual trial itself. Typically, they are worried about compromising their case. But on the flip side, there are a growing number of lawyers who are very sophisticated media-wise. They know that developing a strong PR-centric communications strategy and tapping into the power of the press can bring even more heft to their cases.

With that said, even though crisis counselors may try our utmost, we certainly do not win every argument we make and sometimes clients are hesitant to go with our recommendations. Sometimes that is because they are relying on lawyers to guarantee their future or the viability of their company. In some instances, clients place their trust in lawyers who are too reticent to publicize their case or don't actually understand how to use the media to best serve the interests of their clients.

That is a potential pitfall that organizations must work to avoid. It often happens when a client selects an attorney with no experience working with a specialized crisis PR firm. Even though they may be brought in for their expertise, crisis PR teams can find themselves lacking access to all the information that they should have, which prevents them from working seamlessly as part of the same team. Those situations can become very problematic, often to the detriment of the client's case.

To illustrate how thorny this issue can become, one case in particular stands out in my mind. Years ago, we were working on behalf of a company when they decided they were going to initiate a lawsuit against a major media outlet. Well, their lawsuit has now been going on for years and has yet to go to trial. It is still slowly winding its way through the legal process.

In the meantime, we are no longer involved since the lawyers never authorized us to do what we do best, which is to fight on behalf of our clients in the press, using the tools available to us.

The problem is, while the organization was sitting on its hands awaiting a trial date, we were not allowed to say anything. We couldn't take the necessary steps to prevail; instead we were forced to scale back our PR activities. It was extremely frustrating because we knew that we could have provided help, but the lawyers were overly concerned that our activities might potentially have a negative impact on the case.

Meanwhile, the revenues of the company have plummeted, and their public reputation continues to tank because the world keeps spinning, and life moves on. What's the story with the media outlet that is the target of the lawsuit? They remain free to act with impunity, running stories regularly that continue to decimate the company's brand.

Unfortunately, the advice some clients still receive from attorneys is essentially this: "We should not litigate matters in the press. We will have our day in court, and eventually justice will be served."

The problem with that argument is that justice may or *may not* be served in court. That assumes that the company has the intestinal fortitude—as well as the deep pockets—to spend a fortune and invest time and energy in pursuing legal recourse that will literally take years to materialize. And only if they win at trial. Business owners, please consider this: by the time your company rolls the dice and is finally vindicated in court, you may not even have a company left.

Teaming Up with Attorneys

To be fair, attorneys have big jobs with a lot of responsibility. Often, they do not have enough hours in the day to both build their cases and also engage full-time with the press. Maintaining media relations may be a tall order, but it is one that is increasingly essential. So, for many attorneys, enlisting a crisis PR agency or consultant who can interface with the media makes sense since the attorney does not have the bandwidth or interest in doing so.

The nation's top crisis managers work closely with law firms on a daily basis, making interaction with attorneys part of their typical daily workflow. Meanwhile, organizations who find themselves involved in legal disputes and in need of PR guidance often use their in-house counsel or the law firm assisting them to secure specialized communications counsel.

However, in the realm of litigation PR, crisis PR firms have to carefully select the clients they agree to represent and those whom they decline to assist. Often, you have to make a judgment call as to whether you really believe your client or not. In my own experience, I have said no to a lot of clients because our team was not confident that they were telling us the truth or being open and honest about what had transpired. We have also declined cases in which someone wanted us to wage ad hominem attacks and character assassination to support their legal actions.

> You can either sit back and absorb blow after blow from your accusers or choose to strike back.

Performing well and accomplishing the desired outcomes in the high-stakes arena of litigation PR all comes down to the idea of pressing the truth. Simply put, you can't sit back and hope and pray that one day you get your day in court and that all your problems will go away. You have to get in the fight and defend yourself.

You can either sit back and absorb blow after blow from your accusers or choose to strike back. Wherever you can, you have to blunt their attacks or sidestep them. Block their opening moves and force them to retreat. And no win is given; each one is earned through preparation, determination, and dedication.

CHAPTER 7

HOW WE RISK OUR LIVES ONLINE

The online world has transformed every aspect of our lives, from how we work to what we buy, how we are entertained, and perhaps most dramatically, how we communicate with family, friends, business associates, and the rest of the seven billion people who share the planet.

Our means of communication are now instant. But the principles that govern our discourse are as old as human nature. And that is where it gets tricky. I will show you what I mean by way of this timeless lesson, whose original source is unknown:

In ancient Greece, Socrates was widely lauded for his wisdom. One day the great philosopher came upon an acquaintance who ran up to him excitedly and said, "Socrates, do you know what I just heard about one of your students?" Socrates replied, "Wait a moment. Before you tell me, I'd like you to pass a little test. It's called the Test of Three."

Socrates continued, "Before you talk to me about my student, let's take a moment to check what you're going to say. The first test is *truth*. Have you made absolutely sure that what you're about to tell me is true?" The man said, "No. I actually just heard about it."

"All right," said Socrates, "you don't really know if it's true or not. Now let's try the second test, the test of *goodness*. Is what you are about to tell me about my student something good?" Replied the other, "No, on the contrary."

Socrates continued, "You want to tell me something bad about him even though you're not certain it's true?" The man shrugged, a little embarrassed. Socrates continued. "You may still pass, though, because there is a third test—the filter of *usefulness*. Is what you want to tell me about my student going to be useful to me?" The man said, "No, not really."

"Well," concluded Socrates, "If what you want to tell me is not true, good, or even useful, then why tell it to me at all?"

How much of what we read or see online could pass Socrates's three-part test? It seems the percentage is diminishing every day.

It's Not Virtual; It's Reality

The job of a strategic communicator is to help people and organizations fight for the truth—to help them deliver the right message to the right people, in the right manner, at the right time. And one of the primary ways to deliver those messages is online. The online medium continues to evolve in ways that can offer tremendous benefits to people, but can also severely harm them.

It's a key concept that cannot be stressed enough, not just for PR people and communicators, but for every single one of us. This subject is so important that a couple of years ago I delivered a TEDx talk titled "How We Risk Our Lives Online." I chose to present in front of the most skeptical, derisive, and difficult audience possible—an auditorium filled with high school students.

As I walked onto the stage and introduced myself, I confessed that while I was excited to be there, I was also sad because many in the room would not like what I was about to say. I knew they would take one look at me, draw their conclusions, and tell themselves, "This guy is old. He is out of touch. Yeah, he may be wearing jeans and sneakers, but he doesn't understand. He is not connected with this modern world that we are living in. Forget about it—and forget him."

But I pressed on, telling them the consequences they could expect if they ignored my message. I tried to soften the blow by employing the word *we* as opposed to lecturing them in the second person. "For some of us, our boyfriends or girlfriends are going to dump us. We're not going to get that job we were hoping to get. We'll end up getting bullied online. We're going to embarrass ourselves; we're going to get trolled—we're going to face some really unpleasant situations."

Not the message they wanted to hear. I quickly pivoted to a more positive outlook: "Now my hope is, for the vast majority of us, the exact opposite will be true. And instead, what we choose to do online and how we present ourselves is going to have lots of positive consequences. We're going to find the internship that leads to that ideal job, that puts us on the path to a career that's interesting and exciting and lucrative and rewarding."

"We're going to connect with like-minded people online who share our values and perhaps even meet the partner we'll spend our lives with. We're going to connect with friends; we're going to find out interesting things; we're going to challenge ourselves intellectually."

That was the reality I presented: the polar opposites of online participation. And there is no sitting on the sidelines; in today's world, you *have* to interact.

Then I served up the main message of my talk: "Now, in just a couple of minutes, you're going to walk out of this room, equipped with a secret that you can harness for good—or for bad. And that secret is if you share with care and post with purpose, you will be better equipped to achieve what you set out to do in your life."

"And the other thing I'd like everyone to think about is the notion that we risk our lives online. In some ways it's shocking to say it, but our online lives may be even more important than our actual real lives. At the very least, they can have an enormous influence on how our real lives turn out."

> Our online lives may be even more important than our actual real lives.

As I scanned the room, I could see they were all paying attention, maybe in spite of themselves, and that made me hopeful. Because while every generation thinks they have all the answers, the truth is that all of us need guideposts to rely upon when dealing with such a powerful and pervasive influence as online communication.

You Are What You Post

Today, more than any other time in history, perception is reality. How we present ourselves makes a difference in how people view us. They draw conclusions about us when we have never actually even met in person. So, we all have a responsibility to be the curators of our online presences, because they will impact the future arc of our lives—both personally and professionally.

Right now, through the vast reach of the internet, we are connected to a network of people that spans not just our schools, our workplaces, our towns, our cities, our states, and our country, but the entire globe. We are connected with people with whom we will never stand in the same space or meet face to face.

And the opinions these people form about us will not be based on any personal conversation; we won't be able to dissuade them of any misconceptions. Instead, they are going to be looking for information without our direct involvement. They will be searching for clues. And where are they going to be doing that? Online, of course.

Share with Care and Post with Purpose

There are two key concepts we all need to bear in mind. And I cannot overstate how critical they are for us to think about. The first is: share with care. What do I mean by that? I am recommending that before we share our information over the internet—whether on a blog or through social media in any of its forms—we need to think about safety implications.

It makes no difference whether we are active on Facebook, uploading videos to sites like TikTok or sharing images or posts via Snapchat or Instagram. We need to think about the content each and every time beforehand. Why? Because unwittingly, we may be revealing information about ourselves, friends, loved ones, or other people we know that could literally put us or them in physical danger.

And the other concept is to post with purpose. By that I mean, before rushing to say whatever is on our minds and enjoying the immediacy and satisfaction that social media provides as a way to express ourselves, we need to instead pause for a moment. We need to count slowly from one to five and reflect on what we are doing before we actually post.

We should make sure that what we are about to put out into the universe serves us well and positions us as we would like to be thought of—not as a hateful or spiteful person, but as someone who is caring and respectful. There are an infinite number of instances where people chose not to take these concepts seriously or did not think of them at all. I will provide you with just a few.

> In the swipe of a finger, we are being defined by the digital footprint we leave behind.

These examples illustrate that in the snap or swipe of a finger, we are being defined by the digital footprint we leave behind. And that, unfortunately, can have far-ranging consequences in our lives for years to come.

First, consider the cautionary tale of the beauty queen crowned Miss Teen USA. At first blush, she so clearly exemplified the model of what many young women aspire to be—if you subscribe to the idea that beauty contests indeed deliver on that premise. For all appearances, she was poised, articulate, smart, beautiful, and talented. And yet, within a short time after winning her title, people began looking through her social media.

And what did they find? They discovered that she had repeatedly used racial epithets on her Twitter feed. It changed the way a lot of people thought about her—whether she was actually an example of the way young women should conduct themselves. She was forced to apologize.

Then think about the plight of a well-respected executive who lost his high-paying job. Why? Because during the State of the Union address, he went on Twitter. The tweet he posted was undoubtedly sent in the heat of the moment. He felt passionately about what he was saying. But his post disparaged the wife of a serviceman who lost his life in a high-risk military operation. He was roundly criticized by people on both sides of the aisle.

There was a big hubbub about the tweet on social media, and you may say to yourself, "Well, it's just social media—no one takes it seriously. No big deal." To the contrary, it had real consequences, because within a couple of days his bio had been removed from his company's website. He was fired, and the company he worked for was forced to release a statement saying that the comments their former employee made did not reflect their values. After many years of service to the firm, he had to clear out his desk.

Next up, reflect on a young man enjoying what many people do in their spare time: playing online games with friends. After the games were over, they went on Facebook and continued their back-and-forth. They were chatting and teasing each other when one of the friends texted that the gamer was crazy. To which he responded, and this is just a paraphrase, not a direct quote: "That's right; I'm so crazy I'm going to shoot up a kindergarten."

I imagine his friends understood the context. They felt they were engaged in some good-natured, harmless banter. They knew that he did not literally mean he intended to open fire on a classroom full of five-year-old children. He said it, though.

And guess what? It wasn't his friends or the people he knew who reported him. A stranger who came across his statement was alarmed by what she had seen and contacted the police. Now mind you, this was within a few weeks of the shooting at Sandy Hook Elementary school. Police at any time should take posts like this seriously, but during that time of heightened awareness, they treated it as an imminent threat.

Officers went to his house. They arrested him. They threw him in jail. He spent months behind bars before facing a trial and the possibility of a long prison sentence for making a terrorist threat. What we do, what we say online, whether we are joking or not, matters. Failing to share with care and post with purpose can have life-altering consequences.

But if you believe these are just random examples and these are the exceptions, not the rule, think again. Because the first place that HR people and prospective employers are looking when considering bringing people into their companies is—you guessed it—online. They're examining the digital footprint to see what that person has revealed about himself or herself.

Someone's digital footprint can yield damaging evidence even when that person is not at fault, as in the case of one former teacher. I say former, because he was actually fired due to a picture posted online. It was seen by one of the parents at the school where he taught. The parent contacted the administration, saying, "I enrolled my child in a Christian school. I found a photo of this teacher posing with alcohol, and I don't think this behavior represents our values. It doesn't set the proper example for our children."

And the administration agreed. He lost his job. But here is the really interesting thing. The teacher never actually posted the photo online. He likely had no knowledge it even existed; it was a photo that was posted years earlier on his wife's Instagram feed. Still, someone within the school community went looking around online and came across the offending photo.

The lesson we should draw here is that it is not just the things that we ourselves post that we have to be concerned about. We also have to consider: *What are other people posting about me?* We all must be mindful of both people we know and those we don't. When you are at a party and someone takes a candid picture of you, what's going to happen with that photograph? Could it come back to haunt you? The answer is pretty clearly—yes.

The Screening Process

Today, every person with a smartphone is a potential reporter. Incidents in the past that would fly so far below the radar that nobody would notice can now suddenly become something seen by everyone. A gesture that is small, insignificant, and most likely unintentional can today be blown way out of proportion. And because a picture is worth a thousand words, something captured on camera can take on much more importance than it should. That's the world we live in now, and we have to be aware of it.

Think of it this way. You would not show up for an interview expecting to get the job wearing flip-flops and a T-shirt with the sleeves cut off while using off-color language. Yet bear in mind that as soon as you apply, the interview is already taking place. As part of the screening process, the hiring manager is combing through the online histories of all applicants to determine who makes the cut. And based on what they find and judge you upon, you may never even get that sought-after interview opportunity.

I can tell you from my own personal experience that this happens. In fact, there have been two occasions in recent years where people's online digital footprint sabotaged career prospects. The first happened while I was working in Washington, D.C. I was looking for a writer and needed someone who was talented and could produce high-level material for members of Congress and other policymakers. This person's skills and integrity needed to be top-notch. One day, I got a résumé with credentials that blew my mind. His cover letter was astoundingly well-written. And I was thinking, *This guy is too good to be true!*

Then I did what every person does in this day and age: I visited a website that you may have heard about called Google. And in a matter of roughly 0.43 seconds, I knew beyond a shadow of a doubt that he was not the right guy for the job.

Because when I Googled him, I found that he had been busted for plagiarism. People had written about it online and in the media. I was not about to bring a plagiarist into our office and compromise the integrity of my organization. His digital footprint did him in.

More recently, a very eager young man clearly saw his future at Red Banyan. When I say he was stalking me, I do not mean in the scary sense, like showing up at my house or wanting to make rabbit stew out of my kid's pet bunny. I mean this guy connected with me on LinkedIn, friended me on Facebook, and followed me on Instagram. He called the office, sent emails, and submitted his résumé with a variety of cover letters. He was demonstrating that he *really* wanted to talk with me about what an asset he could be to our company.

Big mistake. Because as a next step, I naturally wanted to see some samples of his work. Admittedly, the writing was pretty good, but by perusing his blog, I found a nasty article disparaging his former employer. And I immediately thought, *Well, that is certainly not someone we are going to hire. His bad judgment and willingness to burn bridges makes him too much of a risk.*

So, where does that leave us? It means all of us, before we share anything online, must remember to do two things: share with care, and post with purpose. We need to hit that pause button and think before we act, and we need to understand that people all around us are going to be drawing conclusions about us.

They are going to take all these different bits of information and put them together like pieces of a puzzle to formulate a picture of who they think we are. Real or not, their perception impacts reality.

At the end of the day, all of us need to consider—not just some of the time or once in a while, but *all* the time—the serious implications of what we share online. And instead of being over-sharers, we should resolve to be more cautious, reserved, and strategic about what we put out into the world.

I sincerely hope that being responsible for our online presence is something we all truly take to heart. After all, our livelihoods, and even our very lives, may depend on it.

PART III

CRISIS CONTROL

CHAPTER 8

CRISIS CAN BE A CATALYST

Although he was better known for revealing the mysteries of the universe, Albert Einstein was also a sage observer of humanity. He once said, "Adversity introduces a man to himself."

Tales of heroism and fortitude abound throughout history. The indomitable British spirit comes to mind during the dark days of World War II. As German bombers unleashed their nightly reign of terror in what was known as the London Blitz, both young and old huddled together in underground tube stations and were told to Keep Calm and Carry On. And they did.

You see the phrase on T-shirts and coffee mugs today, because it remains relevant. Those who persevere will ultimately prevail. More recently, just look at the number of successful startups that were founded in the aftermath of the Great Recession of 2008. Some, like Groupon, Venmo, Slack, Instagram, Pinterest, and Uber are now household names, and their services have become essential to the way many of us conduct our daily lives.

I'm also sure that at some point during their infancy, each was told, "Forget it; this idea of yours will never work."

That unique character trait to defy the odds is nothing less than the story of civilization. No great achievement, whether it's a monumental building or an enduring system of government, could ever be formed without the irrepressible will to see it through to completion. But no one ever said it would be easy.

The Virtue of Adversity

> A time of crisis affords individuals—and companies—a rare occasion to speak out and have people actually listen to what they have to say.

When you find yourself in a tough situation, you must always remain aware of the fact that there is a potential upside as well. You may have to search hard to find a silver lining, but keep looking and it will be there.

More often than not, that silver lining will shine through as a result of your actions. Think of it this way: a time of crisis affords individuals—and companies—a rare occasion to speak out and have people actually listen to what they have to say. This is in contrast to business as usual, when the biggest challenge is typically breaking through the tremendous amount of noise that's out there.

During a time of crisis, you don't have that same problem, because everyone is paying attention. And that alone creates opportunity. We saw this situation in abundance during the coronavirus pandemic.

COVID-19: A Global Case Study in Crisis

As crises go, this was it: the Big One. The one we all feared. Or, at the outset, the one we didn't fear at all, which made its effects that much worse.

A major misconception that crisis managers try to debunk at every turn is the false belief that a crisis is an unpredictable freak occurrence that comes out of nowhere. In nearly every instance, as with the COVID-19 coronavirus, that assessment is dead wrong.

For years, leading experts in America sounded warnings about the devastation a viral pandemic would wreak upon our country and the entire, interlinked global community.

In 2018, speaking at a symposium hosted by the Centers for Disease Control, infectious disease specialist Dr. Luciana L. Borio spoke in stark terms of the danger ahead: "Influenza is a priority to the White House and represents both a health security and a national security threat," she said. "Today, however, we cannot respond with the speed that we need to."

At the time she made this statement, Dr. Borio was serving as director for medical and biodefense preparedness on the National Security Council. But by the time a vast audience was taking her words to heart, that position no longer exists. In fact, her entire unit—the Directorate for Global Health Security and Biodefense—had been eliminated. It was a fateful decision that clearly contributed to America's needlessly slow initial response to this health, security, and economic disaster.

But even had the department been left intact, the American government was not adequately prepared to protect all of us. Which is precisely what makes the TEDx talk delivered by Microsoft founder

Bill Gates in 2015 entitled "The Next Outbreak: We Are Not Ready" so incredibly painful to watch today.

A Pandemic Preview

In his prescient presentation, Gates forecast with eerie accuracy the situation that materialized. He described how a global pandemic had supplanted nuclear war as the most likely mortal threat to large swaths of the world's population.

Gates contrasted the comparatively well-contained Ebola virus with a new doomsday scenario in which people exhibiting no physical signs of illness boarded planes and spread a highly contagious virus all across the world. He introduced a computer-generated model showing each continent blanketed by a deadly virus "spread through the air." It was as if he was giving us a glimpse into a crystal ball.

Gates, whose foundation has dedicated itself to making a momentous health impact worldwide, called years ago for us to build a solid response system utilizing technology that already existed. He spoke about the need to harness advances in biology to rapidly produce treatments and vaccines.

He suggested replacing war games with "germ games" to simulate crisis scenarios, as well as creating a medical reserve corps ready to go at a moment's notice in coordination with the military. Citing a World Bank estimate, Gates warned, "If we have a worldwide flu epidemic, global wealth will go down by over three trillion dollars, and we would have millions and millions of deaths."

In fact, these "germ games" did actually take place. Launched by the Obama administration, pandemic simulation scenarios devised by the Department of Health and Human Services revealed in no uncertain terms how shockingly unprepared the nation was to endure such a crisis.

An extensive exercise was also prepared for the incoming Trump administration, whose federal agencies continued contemplating a potential outbreak. Incredibly, less than a year before the crisis struck, an extensive germ simulation called "Crimson Contagion" was conducted simultaneously in Washington, D.C., and twelve states, including New York and Illinois.

At least a dozen federal agencies participated, including the Departments of Defense and Veterans Affairs and the National Security Council, as well as organizations including the American Red Cross, health insurers, and major hospitals such as the Mayo Clinic. But with that said, most of the planning and thinking behind the effort was developed several bureaucratic levels below the president's cabinet.

And while the secretary of state, director of homeland security, and other high-ranking officials were involved in the exercise and viewed the simulated projections with concern, they had either been dismissed or already moved on from their duties when the first cases of a real virus appeared in early 2020.

Turning Crisis into Opportunity

Companies found that working through the prolonged period of crisis and uncertainty presented by COVID-19 gave them a chance to connect on a different level with all their audiences—employees, partners, the public, and above all, their customers.

In the first weeks of that unprecedented time, most people's inboxes were flooded with messages from organizations of every kind reaching out to provide reassurance and perhaps spark sales during a period of near total economic shutdown.

I'm sure that mystery contacts and companies that you've never heard of sent you emails just to check in and offer moral support. Yes, in some cases they used the occasion to hawk their wares, but many sent communications that expressed, "I just wanted you to know that we are here for you."

Smart companies used the pandemic as an opportunity to demonstrate their responsiveness to their clients. In a service business especially, the strength of the relationship with your client is everything. Those who communicated with their clients on an ongoing or even daily basis and provided assistance during a moment of real need made themselves indispensable.

Maintaining personal connection in trying times is essential. It's as true for crisis PR consultants as any other business. It's true also for B2C (business-to-consumer) companies. If they are smart, then they are always looking for ways to better communicate with audiences of consumers and prospects. So, in the midst of the coronavirus crisis, marketers were given the rare chance to reconnect with existing and potential customers in a meaningful way.

A Blessing and a Curse

During the coronavirus outbreak, our country and many others across the globe were buffeted by negative repercussions far beyond the realm of anything we had ever experienced. Loved ones died. Students missed school. Parents lost jobs. Businesses were forced to shut down, some for good. Entire industries faltered. And medical professionals were stretched beyond capacity. The emotional and financial hardships caused by the coronavirus were immeasurable.

At the same time that it exacted a terrible human toll, the COVID-19 pandemic also provided a chance to reset how people treat one another and communicate during times of need and shared pain. History will be the judge of whether or not we ultimately succeeded in using this jarring event to fundamentally reshape our lives and dialogue in a way that promotes, rather than impugns, our moral character.

We should recognize that the coronavirus pandemic was a unique moment in time where the global community was called upon to come together. And to forge a lasting legacy from that experience, my own hope is that it will have served to rekindle our pursuit of truth and underscored the importance of honest and transparent communication from leaders entrusted with our lives, health, and well-being.

Rethink, Reset, Reinvent

Another unintended, but beneficial, consequence of the COVID-19 pandemic was that it gave people in business a rare chance to thoroughly analyze and reset their efforts. I'll give you an example involving a business owner whom I mentor with a coaching call every month.

He manufactures products, and while he's usually preoccupied with a hectic daily schedule, the virus put an abrupt halt to all that. Because of the pandemic, his production was completely shut down.

It wasn't deemed essential. But because of this downtime, he was given an opportunity to prioritize some core aspects of his business, such as strengthening the systems and processes that he will need to grow and scale. When something upsets routine, it forces a sense of reckoning because it brings about situations in which you have to recalibrate your company. It can change your thinking not only about the way you do business but also about how it fits into your life.

The COVID-19 pandemic gave business owners perhaps more time on their hands than they wanted, but if they used that time properly, it also allowed them to strengthen their fundamentals to stay viable. A lot of companies had to either reinvent themselves completely or go out of business. The nimble leaders saw the silver lining; the terrible outbreak and health crisis actually opened up new opportunities for them.

Consider the case of the CEO of a promotional products company, whose focus was mainly centered on event planning. During the lockdown and the many months following it, there were no in-person gatherings. And since conferences were canceled, there was no need to purchase the giveaways that were the bread and butter of his business. So, what did he do?

A natural wheeler and dealer, he made the most of his skills and hustle as a people person, and he pivoted. Practically overnight, he transformed his company into a business that sourced emergency medical supplies and personal protection equipment. He then connected those suppliers with customers and consequently took a fee for brokering the deals.

It would have been easy to be demoralized given that his core company was decimated. Instead, he created a whole new business and revenue stream that helped him pay his bills and employees, all while taking an active role in helping battle the coronavirus.

Crisis Is a Call to Action

If necessity is the mother of invention, then crisis is the angry father spurring you to action.

Crisis is a catalyst. That is true for organizations of every size and description. It forces them to make big decisions and confront who they really are. By that I mean if a company engenders a crisis due to neglect, bad business practices, or questionable actions by its executives or employees, then it exposes them, and they will have only one of two ways to go.

> If necessity is the mother of invention, then crisis is the angry father spurring you to action.

One route is to embrace, accept, and own up to what they have done and then create the processes for change. That's step one. Next, they need to commit themselves publicly and privately to making those changes and improvements moving forward. Those are the companies who survive crises and live to see another day. They are willing to walk the talk: professing to have strong values and then acting accordingly.

The other is the quicker, easier, but far less effective route. It is taken by companies who try to navigate a crisis by avoiding the issue, being evasive, or not fully accepting responsibility. Those are the ones who will not be able to weather their troubles over the long term. Their brand equity will crumble because people will remember they made the wrong selection when the chips were down. Everyone will see that when confronted with the choice to do what was right or what was expedient, they chose the wrong one.

When those companies, or their chief executives, are unwilling to change during a time of crisis, a change will be made for them. It will be made by their *former* customers.

What *Not* to Do: Lessons from the Top

When a crisis flares up, the protocol for a chief executive should not be too hard to follow. The logical sequence for a person in charge would be to take a step back, impartially assess the situation, and then deliver a thoughtful, measured response. Yet you would be surprised how often the exact opposite happens. Instead, the leader inadvertently serves up a recipe for disaster.

Exhibit A for this type of behavior involves the Lululemon brand and its founder, Chip Wilson. Widely credited with popularizing the athleisure trend in the early 2000s, Wilson turned his company into a billion-dollar fitness-wear sensation that seemingly could do no wrong.

But not so fast. Since those early days, Lululemon has endured a series of self-inflicted crises, none more glaring than the see-through yoga pants scandal. It turned out that the material used for making the company's signature black Luon yoga pants was too sheer. This fact was made very apparent whenever the customer would settle into a downward dog or any other vulnerable position, unwittingly striking a pose that could more aptly be named the full moon.

As you could imagine, when the scandal was revealed (pun intended), the internet blew up; a luxury brand company selling pricey transparent pants was just too ripe for parody. So, in the midst of getting all sorts of bad press, the founder agreed to an interview on TV.

And unfortunately, instead of apologizing to his customers for all the problems they were having, he actually *blamed* them by saying his pants "don't work for certain women's bodies." Adding fuel to the controversy's fire, he then stated, "You know, it's really about the rubbing through the thighs, how much pressure is there, over a period of time and how much they use it."

It was a cringe-worthy moment with consequences for the accomplished entrepreneur. He followed up by essentially saying, and I'm paraphrasing here, "We're an aspirational brand and our products are made for those who are fit, not fat."

Not good. Without question, Wilson's words created even more backlash against the company, and ultimately the board of directors removed him from his leadership role.

Despite being the architect and driving force behind truly staggering success, having catapulted Lululemon to a first-class, global luxury brand, Wilson lost his job in part because he mishandled a crisis situation. He said things that seemed out of step with values the brand claimed to embody. Keep in mind, when you visit a Lululemon store and purchase a $90 sports bra or $100 pair of yoga pants, they hand them to you in a little bag that's covered with affirmations like "Breathe," "Be the change you want to see in the world," and "Friends are more important than money."

In the face of all that positivity, what did you have? A stark contrast between a company proclaiming humanistic values and a CEO who erred by failing to accept responsibility for a mistake that could easily have been explained and rectified. Instead, he placed the onus on his customers, which was a catalyst for Lululemon rethinking its direction as a business. They were forced to confront where they wanted to go and how they planned to get there—in this case, without him.

Being Uber Careful

When talk turns to companies that have become victims of their own success, Uber serves as a poster child. Seemingly overnight, the global ride-hailing company took a revolutionary premise and turned it into a category-defining juggernaut. Yet, this meteoric rise came at a price. Uber was guilty of taking too many unnecessary risks, and for a long while, they got away with them.

But over time, a number of these troubling issues snowballed into full-fledged crises for the ride-share giant. CEO Travis Kalanick was the unwitting star in a harmful display of bullying. Incriminating videos of him berating an Uber driver surfaced, captured by the driver's own camera and then uploaded to the internet for all the world to see. The company was further criticized for privacy invasions, including gathering data on customers without their knowledge or permission.

Other incidents and persistent accusations of a toxic "bro culture" and bad business practices kept cropping up with alarming regularity. Public perceptions shifted from tolerating Uber's antics as a harmless byproduct of an aggressive and brash young CEO to widespread criticism culminating in a movement to #deleteuber and use their competitors instead. The company, said critics, was run more like a college fraternity than a major corporation, and it was certainly not one of high values or upstanding morals.

But you can't laugh off such transgressions as mistreatment of employees and spying on customers forever. The truth will eventually come back to bite you, and with new evidence of impropriety being reported on an almost daily basis, Uber's brand image became tarnished, and the unicorn's gallop began slowing as its ridership numbers began to falter. To their credit, the company's board ultimately decided they needed to go in a different direction.

In the end, crisis—or more accurately a series of them—was the catalyst that forced Uber's board of directors to ultimately dismiss their CEO. To me, the change in leadership signaled recognition of a tested business adage that "what got you here won't get you there."

It is important to understand that Uber likely could never have grown into the behemoth it is today without the bold thinking and relentless hustle of Kalanick. Since day one, Uber was faced with immense legal and other hurdles that would have led nearly everyone to consider the odds long and potentially not worth the fight, given that success was far from guaranteed.

But the young company, led by Kalanick, adopted a fearless and feisty approach, often forging ahead in the face of opposition from entrenched interests committed to the status quo and antiquated laws that never accounted for its revolutionary model. The odds for survival would have been slim, but they were guided forward by a bold CEO fixated on success who just didn't care what the law said.

In his mind, he likely thought, *The laws are antiquated; to hell with them, and we'll figure it out later. We're going to grow.* This win-at-all-costs mentality took Uber from a cool, unproven concept and never-attempted idea and made it real, building Uber into a global brand and forever upending the entire world's approach to transportation.

Ironically, the same total commitment to success that enabled Uber to gain stature within the investor community and ultimately raise nearly $25 billion in capital bled into a managerial style that became a liability. The visionary CEO who was pivotal to igniting the company's initial success was not the right person to lead the mature, publicly held business.

Arguably, his removal propelled Uber into its next phase. It took a series of crises to reveal that truth in stark terms.

Redemption Awaits

> Those who deny problems and are unwilling to take steps to change are the ones who do not weather crises.

Just because a personal or institution-wide crisis is made public does not mean that all is lost. If those at fault try to make amends for their misdeeds and are sincere about it, they can take advantage of a uniquely American character trait. The fact is, we are a very forgiving society. And while the press and public seem to revel in watching the mighty fall, we also love a good redemption story.

People make mistakes—every single one of us—because we are all human and none of us is infallible. And most of us can come back and fully recover from crises, provided we handle ourselves the right way. Those who do not, and who double down and thumb their noses at their peers, only have themselves to blame.

When individuals and institutions are perceived as shirking accountability, or when they fail to understand why they are in trouble, the situation just gets worse. Those who deny problems and are unwilling to take steps to change are the ones who do not weather crises.

That is largely because people have very little tolerance for those among us who are so arrogant that they won't admit or recognize that they have made mistakes, let alone learned from them. If you demonstrate that you are not even willing to humble yourself and pledge to change, then you're not the kind of person that people will be in a rush to forgive.

When Crisis Gets Personal

A prime example of someone who threw away his chance at forgiveness was Anthony Weiner. A married man in a prominent role, Weiner was involved in a series of "sexting" scandals with a number of women, one of whom was underage. These incidents came to light during and after his time in the House of Representatives and being touted as a rising star in the Democratic party. His was a classic case of the old saw: "Fool me once, shame on you; fool me twice, shame on me."

Yes, people will forgive someone who messes up and atones for it. But when you ask for forgiveness and then you repeat the offense, you dig your grave as far as reputations go. And with multiple transgressions after vowing to end his online sexcapades, Anthony Weiner buried any chance of redemption.

To give you the CliffsNotes version of his crisis, the aptly named Weiner literally got caught with his pants down on Twitter after he sent out a link to a revealing picture of himself for all the world to see. He initially lied for several days, claiming that his account had been hacked and that he was not the man in the photo.

"I didn't send it," he said in one televised interview. "I've made it very clear I did not send the picture—that my Twitter account had been hacked," he said in another. When additional photos of Weiner in his birthday suit emerged, including ones that showed his face as well as his physique, he was forced to call a press conference and finally reveal the truth.

Wiping away tears, Weiner confessed to inappropriate involvement with half a dozen women on various social media platforms and over the phone: "I have made terrible mistakes that have hurt the people I care about the most, and I'm deeply sorry," said Weiner. "I have not been honest with myself, my family, my constituents, my friends and supporters, and the media."

Before fielding questions from assembled reporters, he stated: "I've done things that I deeply regret…and for that I'm deeply sorry. I apologize to my wife and our family, as well as to our friends and supporters. I'm deeply ashamed of my terrible judgment and actions."

Weiner's press conference took place on June 6, and by June 16 he had resigned his seat in Congress. And when those lies were initially exposed, he begged forgiveness. He said it was an aberration. He made a mistake. While there were many people who wrote him off immediately, there were others, including his wife, who gave him a second chance.

But when there was still a chance for a glimmer of redemption, he did not change his ways. Two years later, during a campaign to become mayor of New York City, it emerged that Weiner, using the name Carlos Danger, had once again been engaging in sexual exchanges with women, including a fifteen-year-old girl. He would go on to lose the mayoral race with less than 5 percent of the vote, get divorced, and ultimately serve time in prison after entering a guilty plea.

By lying outright as the crisis erupted, he harmed his credibility. But it was the hubris of running for office again while continuing the behavior that got him in trouble in the first place that proved to be his downfall. He had asked for forgiveness only to brazenly turn around and show that anyone willing to give him a second chance was a sucker. Through his actions, he ensured that his name will forever be synonymous with scandal, embarrassment, and inappropriate behavior. He'll never come back.

Yet his story has an ironic twist. It involves the little-known fact that, as part of his comeback plan, he actually got a job at a company that billed itself in part as a crisis management firm. Let's just say his tenure was short-lived. Within a week or two, the firm received such bad press they had no choice but to dump him. Incredibly, the firm actually thought it was a good idea to hire a public figure who completely bungled his own crisis response.

Sex Often Gives Birth to Crisis

Sex scandals have been a constant feature in politics dating back to time immemorial. But sex, that primal urge that makes the world go 'round, can also create crises for "regular" people everywhere. Blame it on human nature, but it can make otherwise rational people behave in ways that are quite the opposite.

This is especially true now that the internet has made it possible to communicate instantly with people across the globe at the same time everyone is carrying around a camera and video recorder in his or her pocket. Ironically, the devices known as smartphones often lead to very unwise behavior.

When people take explicit photos or share intimate material over the internet, they can quickly find themselves "exposed" to crisis situations. And when you throw the coronavirus into the mix, a person can suddenly wind up in very compromising situation. Without going into too much detail about a case that we handled, I'll explain what I mean.

During the midst of the COVID-19 quarantine, our phone rang, and there was a panicked voice on the other line. "I've got a big problem and need help right away." He wasn't kidding.

The problem arose when an individual we will call "Gary" was approached by an attractive woman on a dating app, who then suggested they chat on Skype. Before an hour had passed, she had disrobed, and he had reciprocated. They made plans to chat again in a few days as they ended their virtual visit.

Five minutes later Gary got an email. Attached was a video of him naked and masturbating, which had been recorded on his Skype call without his knowledge. The thrust of the email was a warning: "This video is going to be sent to all your contacts, including your family members, business contacts, friends, and customers unless you wire $20,000 into an offshore bank account within twenty-four hours."

> Even very smart people can do some very dumb things when sex enters the equation.

He was being blackmailed, and this was a huge problem given that he was a respected, well-known leader within the community. If that private video became public knowledge, there was no way his reputation would survive.

When I took his call, he was freaking out. He had gotten some very bad guidance from other people and was about to take a series of steps that would have made things infinitely worse, which he was urged to forget.

We hung up, and a few minutes later, he called back enlisting assistance. I won't go into the particulars about how we worked through his crisis, but in the end, the sextortion failed. Through our counsel, consequences were minimized, and nobody ever found out about the incident. Just chalk this up as a cautionary tale of how even very smart people can do some very dumb things when sex enters the equation.

Digging a Deeper Hole

Bad decision-making often finds its way into the C-suite. You would think that elected officials or corporate executives would have reached their positions of prominence based on their sound judgment and strength of character, but this is not always the case. In fact, when faced with a crisis situation, they very often show their true colors.

As crises go, Deepwater Horizon will forever be known as an all-time example. It's little wonder that a blockbuster movie was made of it. But the event itself was all too real. On a massive British Petroleum (BP) oil rig called Deepwater Horizon located approximately forty-one miles off the coast of Louisiana, a surge of natural gas blasted through the structure's concrete core and ignited the platform, killing eleven workers and injuring seventeen.

Compounding the tragedy, the rupture caused torrents of oil to discharge into the Gulf of Mexico, ultimately totaling more than 3.1 million barrels and coating 1,300 miles of coastline in sticky black goo. As millions watched across the world on a live feed from an underwater camera, the oil flowed unimpeded, and it seemed there was nothing anyone could do to stop it. Finally, nearly three months later, a process that pumped cement through an underwater channel permanently sealed the leak and brought the saga to a close.

We all know that accidents happen, sometimes even on a huge scale such as an unchecked oil spill. If there was ever a time for the BP organization to be sincere and apologetic, this was it. An immediate and heartfelt response could at best strike a sympathetic chord with the public. They would never forget, but at least they could empathize with their plight.

But that's not how the CEO of British Petroleum, Tony Hayward, chose to handle it. One month after his employees lay dead on the platform, and as TVs across the world showed toxic chemicals poisoning the Gulf of Mexico and its wildlife, Hayward was being interviewed on the golf course. And when asked about his company's role in the incident, he did indeed apologize for the "massive disruption."

But then, in the same breath, he added, "Look, there's no one who wants this to be over more than I do. I'd just really like my life back."

Talk about bad optics. As the public face of the oil giant, he would have been hard pressed to come up with a more callous response. In fact, Hayward was then forced to apologize for his apology. It was not exactly how you demonstrate empathy and authenticity. Weeks later, he was quietly ushered out of the job by BP.

The Art of the Apology

Hayward's apology was a disaster in itself. As with anything else, there are both right and wrong ways to accomplish this task. It is a topic that begs examination because at some point in our lives, we all have to do it—or at least we should. For many of us who have been married for decades, the ability to deliver a proper apology is likely something that we have perfected and benefited from immensely. The only difference is how big your intended audience will be. In some ways, a one-on-one apology can be much more difficult than one broadcast to the world. A person who knows you all too well can tell how sincere you are.

In truth, there has probably never been a better time to apologize than the present day; and less of an excuse if you botch it. That's because we have technologies and tools at our disposal that were unthinkable in years past, such as the smartphone, which allows anyone to quickly and easily record an apology and broadcast it. It allows you to tailor your message exactly the way you want and then put it out there for the world.

A decade ago, a person living in the public eye or a senior executive who needed to apologize would likely have done so in written format or assembled a press conference. Logistics and outreach were required. Now, it is literally as simple as pointing, shooting, and uploading; there's nothing to it.

The other reason why a video apology, even if just recorded on a cell phone, can be so effective is that it is primarily visual. By contrast, an apology shared online in the form of a social media post, official statement, or press release does not give people a chance to see you. With a video apology, you can convey the same carefully crafted words, while also using the setting, your body language, and facial expressions and turning these visual cues to your advantage. Done right, a mea culpa on video can be that much more compelling and believable than mere words on a screen or piece of paper.

Sorry, Not Sorry

What is an example of a wrong way to apologize? Obviously, coming across as self-centered, indifferent, or inauthentic does not work. Another failed strategy is the nonapology apology, which is becoming more prevalent these days. It generally is served up as something like this: "I'm sorry if you were offended by what I said."

This formulation typically fails because it puts the onus on the person who is receiving the apology. It implies that you believe they chose to be offended or that it's their fault you are being forced to apologize. By contrast, "I'm sorry for what I said or did," is a way to accept responsibility and own the mistake.

Another option is to never apologize at all. Not everyone can pull this off, but some public figures have such a loyal following they can actually take this approach and make it work.

Martha Stewart is a prime example. She never really gave a formal apology for her insider-trading conviction. She chose not to get into the details and own what she did, and ultimately, it did not matter much for her. She was able to come out of jail as a convicted felon and essentially pick up where she left off. It took a little time, but she remains a household brand—tarnished, yes, but plenty intact.

It may not be fair, but celebrities often have more leeway in this regard than the average person. A-listers who apologize correctly can often get back on track right away. And if their brand is strong enough, even if they botch their response, they will still survive. After all, their fans usually include a core constituency ready to take their side regardless of what they say or do.

No One Goes It Alone

Although credited as being the first man to reach its summit, Sir Edmund Hillary did not scale the peak of Mount Everest by himself. He needed a guide, someone who was content to play a supporting role but knew the treacherous terrain like the back of his hand.

In much the same way, going it alone during the crucible of a crisis can be a very risky venture. You have to be sure that your next move is the right one, because one misstep could lead to peril, dealing a severe blow to you or your organization's reputation long-term.

When faced with the ultimate challenge, Hillary relied on his trusted Sherpa Tenzing Norgay. Similarly, at a time when circumstances may be spiraling out of control or when risks abound, the guidance of an informed and engaged crisis counselor can prove invaluable.

CHAPTER 9

ENGAGING
WITH REPORTERS:
DOS AND DON'TS

The influence of the media is pervasive. And powerful. In a country that cherishes freedom of the press, even at a time when it seems to be under constant assault, there isn't much that can escape the watchful eye of the Fourth Estate. Although we live in a twenty-four-hour news cycle, we seldom stop to think of all the reporting legwork and deadline writing, editing, and fact checking that goes into the stories we absorb on a daily basis.

There is no getting around it. If you want to advance your agenda, correct misinformation, or deliver your intended messages to the outlets that matter most, you have to cultivate a sound working relationship with reporters. Sometimes, the give-and-take between a reporter and a PR professional seems like a well-choreographed dance. Each has a role to play, with certain professional boundaries that should only be breached as a last resort.

The nature of the relationship between members of the media and those tasked with interacting with them is ever-evolving. However, I would like to convey some helpful hints and time-tested approaches when it comes to dealing with reporters. While applicable to most situations involving media engagement, including promotional PR or actively seeking publicity, these tenets become even more relevant in a time of crisis.

> Crisis PR requires artful media relations while a clock counts down ominously to potential detonation.

In effect, crisis PR is regular PR but with much more intensity. Crisis PR requires artful media relations while a clock counts down ominously to potential detonation. It's regular PR and media relations on steroids.

Playing by the Rules

As a crisis PR practitioner, you are typically under more scrutiny, the time frames are shorter, and the margin for error is slim to none. That is why achieving mastery of journalistic best practices is paramount. These guidelines will work in your favor during the best of times but will serve you even better in a volatile situation. So first let's talk about the don'ts, especially one in particular.

Don't Lie

Most of us have been taught from our youngest days to tell the truth. It shouldn't bear repeating as a recommended best practice, but sadly it does, because we are living in a time when lying to the media and the public has become routine. In this day and age, it's almost counterintuitive to advise telling the truth, because lying has become something we don't simply tolerate; it's what we now expect. Lying is definitely not the best way to work with the press, for various reasons. For starters, in the short term you will be found out. And it will happen quickly, because true to the nature of our instant-information society, facts can easily be checked.

What's more, if you say something that is demonstrably false, it will be revealed as such, and the reporter will not take kindly to being lied to or misled. It falls under the category of simple human decency. No one likes to be conned or feel that they've been taken advantage of, just as no one wants to be the target of misinformation. So, lying is a definite no.

And aside from the short-term impact, the long-term implications of falsehoods are even worse. Once you have destroyed your credibility with a

> **Simply put, lies burn bridges.**

reporter, then it becomes that much harder to ever be taken seriously or to be viewed again as a credible source. After all, from a reporter's point of view, if you lie about one thing, then you may lie about everything.

Simply put, lies burn bridges and are credibility killers that call into question the veracity of everything you may have told that reporter in the past, not to mention moving forward.

For a public example of that, look no further than the short-lived spokesman for the Trump White House, Press Secretary Sean Spicer. Mere days after the inauguration, Spicer stood at the podium and uttered the bald-faced lie that the ceremony drew the biggest crowd that had ever attended a presidential inauguration, period.

It was a demonstrably false statement. There was photographic evidence that proved otherwise. For comparison, all one had to do was look at the side-by-side video from previous inaugurations. By any measure, what he said was not true. From that day forward, Sean Spicer never had credibility with the press corps in part because he was caught in a blatant lie about something that was so easily disproved.

After hearing a lie about an event that was relatively inconsequential, how could any reporter be able to trust him to provide accurate information on matters of real importance? They couldn't. Spicer became a liability, and he was eventually replaced.

Setting the Record Straight

Now we have established that it's never a good idea to lie to a reporter. But what if you have sensitive information to pass along to a reporter but don't necessarily want to be named as the source? What are the protocols for speaking on the record, off the record, and somewhere in between?

Generally speaking, there are three main approaches to take. The first one is "on the record." If you are a reporter, a conversation that takes place on the record means you can attribute what I say directly to me by name. In other words, you can use anything and everything I'm telling you, and you can tell the world that I said it. That's on the record.

"Off the record" is supposed to mean that you cannot attribute the information to me, nor can you identify me in any way, shape, or form, or even use what I told you in your reporting. Off the record is meant to be protected communication treated with total confidentiality.

In fact, in conversations that are off the record between a source and a reporter, journalistic ethics demand that a reporter respect that critical confidentiality. Revealing what came out of an off-the-record conversation and who provided it amounts to what's termed "burning a source."

Burning a source entails a reporter using information that he or she is not supposed to use or using it against the source's wishes. It is an enormous violation of journalistic ethics, because it can lead to serious consequences for the source. It also damages the credibility of the reporter in the same way being caught in a lie damages the credibility of a source.

Just as I would advise people not to lie to reporters, I implore reporters not to burn sources. After all, once a reporter displays a willingness to burn one source, why should anybody ever trust that reporter again? Lying to a reporter or being betrayed by one—I see it as two sides of the same coin.

But you should also keep in mind that between these two absolutes—"on the record" and "off the record"—there are subtle nuances. For example, one reason you might want to say something off the record is because you're trying to provide information to a reporter to help him/her better understand the context. Even if you have provided information that the reporter cannot use, you have ideally made an impression and in some fashion impacted the journalist's thinking.

It's a tactic similar to the one employed by a courtroom lawyer who makes a statement in front of the jury that produces an objection from the other side that is sustained by the judge.

The attorney said something that left an impression on the jurors, and they can't unhear it, even if the judge instructs them to disregard it. That's akin to what happens sometimes when you provide information off the record to a reporter.

Speaking off the record doesn't always have to involve slick maneuvers. You may simply want to alert a reporter about a pressing issue or guide them toward a story without inserting yourself into it. One reason could be that you don't want them to feel like you have an agenda. Or you don't want it revealed that you're involved in this issue, but you think it is something the reporter and the public should care about.

One important thing to keep in mind when speaking with a reporter off the record is that there's always a chance you could get burned. So proceed with caution, even when you believe you have an agreement. When speaking off the record, you have to make certain that you and the reporter are in agreement that what you're saying is confidential and not attributable.

The way you do that is by explicitly setting the parameters for the conversation itself. By that I mean you can never just presume that you are off the record; you need to secure agreement from the reporter confirming that, indeed, you are. My biggest piece of advice is this: make sure you have confirmed that you are off the record before you start running your mouth.

For a harsh lesson in what can happen when you fail to do so, feel free to Google the interview in the *New Yorker* with short-lived White House Communications Director Anthony Scaramucci. And of course, it follows that if you're engaging with a reporter you don't really trust, you run a big risk by merely saying the conversation is off the record and then hoping they will comply.

A more secure way to avoid miscommunication and ensure that whatever you provide is truly off the record is to demarcate it as such and put it in writing. When you email, you create an electronic paper trail. It's an effective safeguard against a reporter burning you, since you stipulated in writing that the information was strictly off the record. That's why it sometimes makes more sense to send a reporter information via email as opposed to communicating it orally.

The Importance of Background

Every single day, there are informed sources who need to protect their personal privacy while giving information to reporters; this falls into a third category called "background."

Allowing a person to willfully share information, and to make it public and have it reported, but without having the source identified, is a vital journalistic practice. Even though a common refrain is to criticize reporters who cite unnamed or anonymous sources, this actually provides a fundamental protection that people often need when going to the media.

The assumption should not be that a reporter who uses an unnamed source is a bad reporter or that they are making things up. Yes, there are famous examples of reporters being humiliated and fired for inventing sources, but by and large, that's an aberration. It's not a common practice, and reporters should not be disparaged simply because their stories cite unnamed sources.

Individuals with important information that benefits the public often require the protection that anonymity provides. Keeping their names out of the story provides a way for them to convey facts through the media without suffering undue consequences, which could be threats either to their careers or to their actual safety.

The most famous example would be Deep Throat from the Watergate scandal. For the integrity of the country, those disclosures needed to get out. And if the reporters hadn't been willing to use information they received from an unnamed source, then the extent of President Nixon's crimes would possibly never have come to light. Just think how different history would have been.

"On background" means you can have a conversation with a reporter, and the reporter can then use the information you give while not attributing it to the source directly. They can quote from it, they can refer to it, but they cannot attribute it to you personally. This provides some flexibility and allows some wiggle room in terms of how you can negotiate with the reporters and how they will characterize the source of their information.

To illustrate how this works, consider the articles you may have read in print or online. Sometimes you will see them written with attributions like, "a source with knowledge of the situation," or "said someone close who spoke on the condition of anonymity" or "someone who was there for the discussions relayed." In such instances, the reporter is protecting the identity of the source who spoke on background.

Negotiate Before You Say It

Often, you can negotiate how you will be referenced before providing a reporter with information. Similarly, there are instances when you can restrict a reporter's use of your account of a story by holding them to an agreement that they're not going to say anything that could potentially reveal you as the source of the information.

Such negotiations between source and reporter can be of paramount importance. For instance, put yourself in the shoes of a whistleblower involved with a company that has done very bad things. If you have evidence that can incriminate them, then it's essential for you to prove what you're telling is true. As the source, you have to give the reporter the raw materials they need in order to write a piece and confirm the authenticity of your information, but you must convey it in a manner that also protects your identity. Being on background is a way to do both.

Keep in mind, there are varying degrees to which reporters understand these nuances and there is no one-size-fits-all solution. Before the facts are ever discussed, communication with the reporter has to be handled in a highly professional way, by someone who knows how to take the lead. That's where the skills of an experienced crisis counselor come in.

You also can't rely on just assuming that the reporters fully know and grasp these concepts. At the most venerated publications, of course they do. If you're talking to a reporter from the *Washington Post* or the *Wall Street Journal* who covers national security or defense, they are intimately familiar with source attribution. They're at the top of their craft, and they work within these parameters all the time.

However, if you're talking to a reporter at a local news station or an outlet that has a less stringent editorial process, such as a blog or smaller publication, it's very important that you discuss the ground rules before you start revealing information on background. You have to engage in a very open conversation with the reporter as to how you both define a background discussion, and then come to an agreement before you start giving them the goods.

When the stakes are high is not the time to be figuring out how to put these concepts to use for the first time. Instead, look to engage an expert in this arena; someone who is used to working with reporters and who can negotiate identity preservation when the stakes are high. Trying this out for the first time when you are facing a critical moment is not advisable.

When your company is under scrutiny, or you're trying to put out information that tells your side of the story, the situation calls for a specialist. You want to speak with one voice and in a way that powerfully conveys your narrative. Whether the crisis you're facing is imminent or in its early stages, you should immediately designate a veteran in dealing with reporters to speak on your behalf. And knowing the press means understanding the rules of engagement. Attempting to simply ignore or bully reporters won't get you the results you're seeking.

History has proven that the pen is mightier than the sword, and media outlets are the gatekeepers of information. Therefore, if you want to make sure your story is told right, then you've got to engage. You have to be willing to create a connection with reporters and press the truth.

Freedom of the Press: A Foreign Concept

Bear in mind, you cannot actually dictate to reporters how they will ultimately write their articles. That may work perfectly well in third-world countries or dictatorships without a free press, but not here.

As a matter of fact, I've counseled foreign leaders operating in the United States who displayed a fundamental lack of understanding of how media works in a free society. I recall a fascinating conversation I had with a foreign diplomat about this very topic. Now understand, this was a senior-level representative working in a foreign embassy in Washington, D.C.

He said to me, "So, you will write the article and then you will give it to a reporter who we pick from the *Washington Post*, right?"

"No," I answered. "That isn't going to be possible, because I'm not a reporter who works for the *Washington Post*. They're not going to let me write a news article for them."

He thought this over, and said, "Aha, okay, I understand now. You will write a story and give it to a reporter. And the reporter will put his name on the story and run it in the *Washington Post*, right?"

I replied, "No, unfortunately, that also will not work." I saw his quizzical expression, so I explained, "Reporters in America write their own stories, and they don't just take pieces written by other people and run them under their bylines. It's just not how it's done here."

He was still perplexed. "So, what do you mean, then? Who will decide the story?"

And I said, "The reporter writes the story. And the editor will decide if the story appears. What we can do as public relations consultants is help them by making a case for the story and providing them with information. But at the end of the day, they're the ones who decide if they're interested in the story and who will put it together. They have an obligation to be fair and to look for input from multiple viewpoints, but in the end, it is their decision."

He shook his head and walked away, probably thinking how life was much easier back in his home country.

We Can Work It Out

That dialogue with a foreign diplomat illustrates a key aspect of news gathering: the importance of having an expert on hand to help a reporter develop a story, especially during a critical time. This collaboration relies heavily on the ability of a crisis manager or media representative to build a mutually beneficial working relationship with the press, because a reporter needs information in order to assemble an article.

Reporters are looking for accurate and credible information, because in the absence of that, they won't have the substantive facts on which to base a story. Otherwise, they'd just be relying on thin air or information that isn't good, which they don't want and which their editors would probably question.

Although it may fall under the broad category of journalism, keep in mind that all reporting is not the same. There's a spectrum of editorial styles, ranging from what's known as "hard news"—fact-driven reporting on current events—to opinion journalism, whereby a writer is given license to weigh in on a topic with their point of view.

Public relations practitioners have to be adept at engaging with a variety of reporters, whose styles and thought processes may be totally different from one another. And part of why you want to hire an experienced PR person is because you want someone who understands these differences and who knows how to work with them accordingly.

On a fundamental level, no matter what their genre is, all reporters need ideas. They want to tell stories, and they want access to interesting topics that are going to resonate with their audiences. PR people can play a critical role in providing news outlets with ideas by bringing stories to light that reporters and feature writers would not otherwise have known about.

So yes, journalists do rely on communications people in order to bring them stories. They don't do so exclusively—many times they come up with their own stories themselves—but there's a mutually beneficial relationship between reporters and good strategic communicators.

Reporters like going to respected PR people because they know they'll be engaged in a way that's very professional and ethical. Such PR pros understand the speed at which the press works, so the reporter can be confident that their PR counterpart is going to get back to them immediately or very, very fast.

Secondly, reporters look for PR people who work with interesting people and newsworthy organizations, because they'll have access to information or enlightening stories that the reporter might want to tell. Above all, there has to be a level of trust, and as a PR professional, you build trust by behaving in an ethical, forthright, and professional manner. Conversely, you eliminate trust when you don't.

Long-term public relations success comes from decades of working successfully with reporters. They need to trust that their source is credible and that the information can be thoroughly vetted. Don't tell lies; don't sell spin; deliver facts.

It also helps to be selective about when you go to reporters, because they should not be bombarded by the same people day in, day out. It's like the boy who cried wolf. If you go to a reporter with every possible story, then you weaken your own credibility because you've just become an annoyance, a dreaded name in the inbox.

You can almost hear the reporter saying, "Oh, my gosh, this person's pitching me again. He calls or writes me every single week." Want to ensure that reporters never listen to you? Pitch them constantly.

On the other hand, when you reach out to producers at national TV shows or top-tier outlets, make sure that you don't waste their time on stories that aren't going to be a good fit. That is how you build trust.

Relationships Made Right

In terms of the relationship between a PR professional and a reporter, an old French proverb comes to mind: "Friends are lost by calling often and calling seldom." You need to strike the right balance between being absent and overdoing it.

You never want to annoy the reporter, and you don't want to come to them with such large gaps in between that they don't remember who you are. You also don't want to constantly contact the media solely to ask for things that help out your agenda alone. Media relationships are like relationships with other people in your life: be a giver and not just a taker.

To be a giver means making their lives easier and being helpful to them, which in turn cultivates an invaluable journalistic contact you can reach out to when needed. But most importantly, it allows you to reframe the dynamic entirely and stop looking through the lens of your needs alone. It's a more natural way to build a relationship that doesn't require expectation of a quid pro quo.

> Deliver information in a way that makes the media's lives easier, not more complicated.

Here's a suggested way to go about it. On a regular basis contact reporters with story ideas or bring interesting people or items to their attention, even when it has nothing to do with your company or a client. For instance, if you have a friend who's qualified to talk about a certain subject, then put them in touch with a journalist and then step aside. Touch base with reporters from time to time just to be useful, to check in and to sow the seeds of trust, which don't take root overnight—or based on a single phone call.

One key thing to keep in mind is to deliver information in a way that makes the media's lives easier, not more complicated. That's how you endear yourself to reporters and make them want to work with you. So, I would put all this relationship-building effort under the category of what you should do, but there are others in my profession who pursue a different approach.

Some people in crisis PR pride themselves on how aggressive they are, bragging to clients about how they berate reporters or leapfrog them to complain to their editors. I fail to see the benefit and think that behaving in such a manner does a disservice to the client. In the course of my career, I can count on one hand the number of times that I've been in a yelling match with a reporter.

Have I advocated forcefully for my client's position? Yes. Have I raised the level of my voice while passionately making the case for why the thesis of a story was off or why the reporter was seeing things through the wrong lens? Certainly, I've done that. But I don't turn our discussions into personal attacks or step over the line of common decency and neither should you.

Remarkably, that sort of behavior is not uncommon in the crisis PR realm. There are a number of people in this space who like to cultivate the image that reporters know not to mess with them. They have no problem being known as someone who tries to bully reporters, or to steamroll and insult them.

Does eschewing those tactics make you a pushover? No. Does it mean that you are willing to let false accusations or false assertions go unchallenged? Absolutely not. Does that mean you are not going to press the truth or not going to fiercely advocate for your clients? Not on your life.

At the end of the day, I am a big believer that you catch more flies with honey than vinegar. Be aware that reporters, and the media outlets who employ them, maintain a level of control whether you like it or not. They ultimately decide if they want to move forward on a piece and, if so, how it will turn out. It makes sense to build cordial relationships with them.

That's why I recommend that you consider taking a confrontational approach only as a last resort. As most of us have learned at home with our own children, losing patience and becoming angry is usually not a good way to get them to do what you want, win them over to your viewpoint, or earn respect. Instead, such tactics often make others harden their positions.

For many who work with reporters every day, it is painful to see the amount of criticism heaped on journalists. In recent years, the profession overall has been disparaged, and it has somehow become acceptable to ridicule reporters, call them fake, or even threaten them verbally or physically. I don't agree with that, because I firmly believe that the press is essential to our democracy. Deliberately undermining its role undermines one of our nation's most cherished freedoms.

Cultivate the Connection

As mentioned, here are some steadfast PR approaches to employ when engaging with reporters. Deal with them openly, honestly, and transparently. Bring them good stories and refrain from bombarding them with items that likely won't be of interest. When pitching a story, avoid being demanding or insistent. Those are principles that never change.

However, the mechanics of how you talk to reporters and literally how you connect with them continues to evolve with each passing year. A big part of it is making sure you meet the reporters wherever they "live." It doesn't matter what your preferred mode of communication is, it is the reporters' preferences that matter. You are the one who has to adjust.

Just because you like to talk on the phone does not mean a reporter wants to get on the phone with you. Many journalists in this day and age don't want to take phone calls because they dread being tied-up in a conversation from which they cannot escape. More often than not, they're on deadline and a ringing phone is seen as a true interruption. It breaks their concentration and derails them from finishing their assignment.

At the same time, there are some reporters who welcome the chance to chat directly, as opposed to trading electronic messages. You have to be willing to go where the reporters are and meet them on their terms. In fact, knowing their preference is the first thing you should establish. In your initial contact with a reporter, you simply ask him or her, "What's the best way to connect? Would you prefer that I email you or do you want me to text you?" It's that easy.

It used to be that calling a reporter was how all business was conducted. Not long ago, email became the principal way to communicate in the workplace. And it was immediately adopted by a majority of reporters, with good reason. One advantage of emailing journalists is that it lets you attach documentation, supporting evidence, and anything else reporters can review on their own.

In recent years, there are a lot of reporters who no longer want email because of inbox bloat. Reporters suffer from information overload, and they literally receive hundreds of email pitches a day. It's almost impossible to break through that clutter unless you pitch them effectively by immediately capturing their interest with a killer subject line or compelling first sentence.

Today, some reporters prefer the immediacy of text messages, with many living on WhatsApp or other platforms. Other reporters live and breathe on Twitter. They operate entirely within the Twitter universe. If you want any shot at connecting with them, then you better be ready to tweet and DM in a limited number of characters. So, it's imperative for any PR practitioner or crisis counselor to know how to use social media and be comfortable with its myriad forms.

> It's imperative for any PR practitioner or crisis counselor to know how to use social media.

Communication constantly evolves, which means that public relations professionals have to do the same. Stories emanate and ultimately come together when various pieces of information are woven together. Today, it's all about "engagements"—that combination of likes, retweets, comments, and other interactions that make up a person's online presence. It's where many stories get told and repeated and "go viral." Social media has rapidly become the essential outlet for anyone seeking to get a story written, seen, and talked about.

An average person may not think about how a story comes together or how it's formulated. But savvy professional communicators can look at any given piece and read between the lines. They can tell with a high degree of certainty where the story emanated, with whom the reporter talked, and where they got their information. They can piece together all the threads.

And as any skilled crisis counselor will tell you, the most important thread in this tapestry is often your connections with reporters.

CHAPTER 10

STICK TO YOUR MESSAGE

Before stepping up to the podium, facing the camera, or firing off an email, there is one essential element every successful communicator must have: a well-thought-out message. And when communicating in a crisis situation, the importance of getting your message right is magnified tenfold.

Messaging is everything. It is the skeleton upon which the entire body of communication relies to provide structure; it's at the core of whatever an organization or an individual is presenting. It is simply impossible to communicate powerfully without clearly articulating a primary message.

In a crisis, that message must concisely convey the key facts and information about a situation. And it should be coupled with an articulation of who you are in terms of your values, what your priorities are, and what action you plan to take.

In the realm of politics, people talk about the necessity of having a good stump speech. That's a colloquial term that harkens back to the early days of our country, when candidates would literally stand on tree stumps to be seen and heard by a gathering of curious onlookers. And the principles of what was said then still hold true today.

A stump speech is, in effect, a fuller iteration of core messaging—the essential communication that a candidate uses again and again, while traveling from place to place, rally to rally. At each event, there are certain key points the office-seeker needs to get across to the audience. And a smart, disciplined politician doesn't deviate from that messaging. No matter how far along on the campaign trail the politician is, the stump speech remains essentially the same.

Stay True to Your Core

Many successful organizations also recognize the value of having a core message that clearly defines who they are. It identifies their mission and purpose not only externally, for their customers and the public, but also internally, for their employees. In crisis situations, that core messaging should include a refutation of any false accusations or flawed reporting. It should also provide an affirmation of your positive attributes as an organization or as an individual.

The very first things that your team will need to fall back upon in a time of crisis are your core messages. This stands to reason, because if you do not know what you want to articulate clearly, then how could you possibly be effective conveying it? Decide what your basic premise should be, and then lock it down. Smart organizations do this during a time of calm, well before any tough situations arise.

Developing your core messages should absolutely involve the person who will be articulating them publicly, whether it be the CEO or a designated spokesperson. And in a time of crisis, the legal team should also be involved. This helps to make sure everything has received a stamp of approval, so that what is said won't jeopardize anyone from the company further down the line.

Just as an example, say there is a deadly accident, and you or your company may be involved in a yet-to-be-determined way. While you want to express your condolences to the family and provide information at the earliest oppor-tunity, you will probably also want to avoid accepting responsibility directly until it becomes known exactly where that responsibil-ity lies. Otherwise, you could be courting liability claims and huge financial consequences.

> At every stage of the communication process you have to think through what you're saying before you say it.

The lesson here is that at every stage of the communication process you have to think through what you're saying before you say it. This cannot be stressed enough. You must make sure that everyone involved is comfortable with the core messaging before you start disseminating it.

Start Spreading the News

And that leads to the next vital question regarding your core messages: How do you disseminate them? Today, the answer is not quite so simple. That's because there are so many more media channels and outlets available to us now than ever before. And each of them has its own idiosyncrasies with which to contend.

By definition, every bit of information you push out should have the same core messages; after all, they are the essence of what you are trying to communicate. But they need to manifest themselves in all the different avenues of communication available to you. That means the same key messages you convey in a press release should also appear on your website.

Your core messages should also be echoed in your social media posts. If you're creating a video, then you want it to rely on the very same messages you worked so hard to develop. And those same messages will be the crux of your argument when you write an op-ed or a letter to the editor. The list goes on.

When you engage with reporters in the context of an interview, the talking points of your core message have to be embedded in every answer you give. They should be the main thrust of your conversation if you organize a press availability. Every time you face the media, you should draw your responses from that same well.

In other words, you must take your core messages, adapt them to the relevant arenas in which they are going to be shared, and use them again and again, across all relevant channels. By putting forth a consistent message, you also benefit from the cumulative effect of having your story reinforced every time someone sees it in a different format.

Consistency is crucial, because it prevents you from saying one thing on one day, and then contradicting it the next, a trap that too many inexperienced speakers fall into. Consistency means making sure you're not leaving anything to chance. It ensures that your message is getting out there, because every opportunity you get, you are conveying the same message.

By channeling your content and always directing conversations toward your core messages, you reduce your margin for error and control the narrative so that you're able to press the truth.

Voicing the same few words over and over again may seem like overkill, but if it's being done artfully, it won't come off as redundant.

Remember your objective: you want your messaging to be persuasive, pervasive, and omnipresent.

That way, whenever people are seeking information about you or the topic you are connected with, they receive the communication you want them to get. And in time, the validity of your message is strengthened, because your core statement is credible and convincing and is being projected from all media outlets.

> You want your messaging to be persuasive, pervasive, and omnipresent.

The Perils of Going Off-Script

Understandably, human nature poses a challenge to this approach. People have an aversion to repeating themselves, and they don't want to be told what to say. I hear it all the time: "Oh, our CEO doesn't like to read from a script. He is a great communicator who prefers to deliver his remarks off the cuff." But when dealing with crisis situations, speaking extemporaneously is almost always a recipe for disaster.

Here is a secret that many people don't know. Good communicators are not those who step to the mic and just let 'er rip. They are people who are absolute masters at scripting what they are going to say in advance but then delivering it in a way that doesn't come off as scripted. Watch in awe as someone walks up to a microphone without any notes and gives great answers during a press conference or delivers a killer speech. What you are seeing is a talented communicator at work.

But what you don't see are the hours of preparation that this person has done to compile the research, taking all the relevant facts into account to determine exactly what the core messaging is going to be before delivering the remarks in a way that doesn't come off as robotic.

Skilled communicators don't have to sound like a broken record using the exact same phrasings precisely because they have done their behind-the-scenes homework. This is what makes their responses appear effortless and empowers them to deliver their messages in a variety of different ways. There is nothing wrong with performing variations on a theme. In fact, this is a good thing.

For a high-stakes interview, the goal is to field tough questions but not answer them verbatim, time and time again. Instead, you should be able to infuse your core messaging in a way that keeps the message consistent but the delivery fresh. That's when you're demonstrating the skills of an effective communicator.

All crisis counselors have encountered clients who tell them: "Our CEO has command of the situation, and he likes his remarks to be spontaneous." While they may acknowledge the need for a core message, they are hesitant to upset their boss, afraid that he or she will be insulted or feel constrained.

I recall a conversation with the staff of a leader facing charges that could put him behind bars and bring down the organization he represents. He intended to go before the media to do a press availability, because he wanted to proclaim his innocence and show that he had nothing to hide.

He felt it was very important for people to see him talk publicly and address his detractors directly. And I actually agreed with that thinking, but I disagreed with their reaction to my proposed next step: "Okay, now we need to prepare a statement for him."

Immediately the pushback began. "No way," they said. It was very definitive. "Our CEO will never read a prepared statement. It's just not his style to read from a script, and he will seem coached and unnatural."

And my response to that was, "Well, that style is part of what got him in so much trouble to begin with." I pointed out that when he previously talked with reporters, he did so without a framework for his answers, and he gave long, rambling answers that were used against him.

I was referring to his prior exchanges with the press where he did not display focus and had not adequately prepared. He failed to drive core messaging, talked in circles, and gave reporters so much content to choose from that they could hand select quotes for their stories that fit their narrative and not his.

I explained that sobering fact to them, saying, "If you had come to me first, I would have told you, 'This is what the answer is going to be.' And we'd have given him two or three sentences, at most to use. Now you're complaining that the reporters cherry-picked their quotes. Of course, they did. Your CEO gave them pages and pages of material. You made it easy for them."

By sending him out to talk unprepared, his team actually gave reporters the rope they used to hang him. In a crisis, less is often more. The CEO should have delivered a very concise and robust refutation of the accusations in a form that was so succinct that it would have been unethical for the reporters to pick apart the quote. Doing so basically forces the media to use such a statement in its entirety.

In many client situations crisis managers have to address past missteps gingerly, while proposing concrete steps to move the situation forward. So, I said, "Why don't we prepare a brief statement for him to read at the beginning? And then, given his style, if he wants to expound upon it, he can do so. But at least in the initial moments of the press conference, when everyone is paying attention to every word he utters, they will all be focused on those exact words, which are the most important."

I knew that in any press conference, the first couple of minutes, actually even the first few *seconds*, are crucial when it comes to getting your core messages across. That's why I implored them to have their CEO deliver a strong, clear, powerfully scripted message prepared in advance so that we could control every word. By doing just that, we dramatically increased the likelihood that our core message would get out, which is exactly what happened.

"What's more," I said to them, "if there are some people who can't stay for the entire press availability, you guarantee that they get a great sound bite right at the beginning. So, they've already gathered what they need in order to do their work as journalists."

While his staff were reluctant, the CEO under fire came to understand the strategy behind the recommendations he was receiving.

I went on, saying, "The talking points will help him communicate his story in a powerful way, because first of all, he'll get help preparing them from a team of experts. And second, they will check all the boxes and make sure that he addresses everything that needs to be covered for this event.

"If he wants to provide flourishes or elaborate upon them when he's up at the podium, that's okay. But at least you'll know he's going to touch on all key topics, and he'll provide focused moments where he'll say exactly what we want the audience to hear."

And they replied, "Hmm ... maybe he would do that. I don't know; let's try it."

The point here is that sometimes people at every level of an organization have a hard time agreeing to a course of action that is actually to their benefit. They don't like relinquishing control or being forced to admit that their previous approach was ineffective. It's bad enough to make a mistake; nobody wants to be reminded of it. No one wants to be proven wrong.

However, in those instances, the crisis counselor has to be persistent. And creative. You need to frame your proposed approach in a way that makes sense. Or better yet, help them see that your thinking is just an extension of their own ideas and the best way to accomplish their goals.

After all, the key to staying on-message is getting the client to employ core messages and then working to deliver them in the most effective manner possible.

Thriving in the Public Eye

For every person who's a natural performer and loves talking in front of a crowd, there are many more who are terrified of speaking in public. A lot of people are unaccustomed to that white, hot glare of the spotlight. Stage fright takes over. Maybe they can speak confidently about themselves in a one-on-one situation, but when they have to speak publicly, it's a totally different story.

Their fear is understandable. That is especially true in times of crisis, when accusations are hurled and the margin for error is nonexistent.

As an extreme example, when you're in a crisis situation and find yourself accused of appalling, horrible things, anything you say can and will be used against you in the court of public opinion. And in this day and age, you can be certain that even seemingly innocent remarks can be twisted to conform to someone's agenda, without your consent.

Keep in mind that video is pervasive. And skillful video editing can make anyone an unwitting victim of deep fakes. Deep fakes occur when fake video or audio files are created to make it look like someone said or did something they actually didn't do. This video manipulation technique is more pervasive online, especially on partisan websites and politically oriented social media.

But nine times out of ten, you don't need to be maligned by a deep fake to become the victim of an incriminating video. All you need to do is go off-script and deliver a long-winded message. By doing so, you allow someone to take that raw footage and edit it in a certain way to make you look guilty of pretty much anything they want.

It's the risk you run if you don't script your statement, especially in cases where you might be facing serious criminal charges. That's because even if they are not true, people have a bias toward believing allegations. Unlike a court of law, where you are innocent until proven guilty, many times if people hear of an alleged crime, or read an accusation in reputable news outlets, their assumption is that it is true.

And that illustrates the challenge that crisis communicators often face. When representing someone who's accused of unsavory actions, you are starting in a place where there has already been a rush to judgment, and that judgment is "guilty." In such instances, crisis counselors have to fight back very aggressively on all fronts, given that they are essentially starting with two strikes against them.

When confronting a crisis, you have to assume reporters and the wider public are approaching you from a hostile viewpoint or with a high degree of skepticism. The default is that people are suspicious of you, and you actually have to prove your innocence with the public rather than waiting for a jury to prove you're guilty. Once you've been accused of something, no matter if the allegation is false or not, you are automatically on the defensive side of the ball.

> When confronting a crisis, you have to assume reporters and the wider public are approaching you from a hostile viewpoint or with a high degree of skepticism.

When that is the case, the calculus has to change. You have to be much more cautious and careful of what you say moving forward. You have to approach every public gesture from a risk mitigation standpoint and limit your exposure to any more accusations. That's why it becomes so important to be extremely disciplined and focused on what you're saying and communicating.

Having a good crisis manager can help you set the terms of any public appearances or media interactions. There are certain rules of engagement for every press encounter, and you should do everything in your power to create an environment favorable to your point of view.

That means you should be looking at ways to drive your narrative and increasing the likelihood that you get your version of the story out, while at the same time limiting the chances that detractors will be able to smear you. Right off the bat, it starts with the words you choose, especially should you decide to hold a press availability.

Do not simply announce that you're having a press conference and leave it at that. Instead, say you are hosting a press conference to "forcefully denounce the false claims brought against you." Doing so helps you drive a message before your event even takes place. If you have a strategic goal for your press conference—and you better— don't let it go unsaid. Put it in there.

When you have an opportunity to communicate the main thrust of your argument, you should leverage your core messaging every chance you get. Every tweet, every Facebook post, every conversation—they should all be geared toward the strategic objective of driving your core messaging, communicating clearly, and getting you through the crisis.

Words matter. The adjectives you choose and how you describe your actions will influence the way people perceive them. That's why a skilled crisis manager might describe how a client will "aggressively defend his reputation" or "will reveal crucial evidence that provides full exoneration" even before you deliver that message yourself. Effective communication goes beyond the basic who, what, when, and where. It presses the truth.

The Essentials of Timing

Timing is another factor to consider when you're getting your message out. Many times, it's advantageous to preempt negative accusations or coverage that you know is coming your way. If you get to the press first and you communicate your story before it's told by others, then you are the one who's providing the context. It's much easier to start painting the landscape than to react to whatever your detractors have already put out.

So, if you've got bad news, tell it first, and tell it all. If you have information to share that exonerates you, that's great. But if it's bad news, telling it first is critically important. It may be painful. It may go against every fiber of your being, but swallow that bitter pill.

Just get it out of the way. Because what you don't want to do is lie by omission or fail to address the full range of negative accusations at the outset. If further accusations keep popping up, it keeps the story in the news cycle. People will continue to talk about it. What's more, if you try to get selective about what you say, and then new information comes out, it harms your credibility.

Whereas, if you address the key areas of controversy right out of the gate and frame them with your explanation, they become old news, which is

> If you've got bad news, tell it first, and tell it all.

what you want. There won't be new allegations creating a snowball effect. You reduce the likelihood that you'll be facing an avalanche of bad news if you make a preemptive disclosure from the start.

In some situations, you're required by law to make certain disclosures. In one such case, I worked with a medical facility that suffered a data breach. Bad actors had circumvented multiple levels of security, and patient confidentiality was compromised. Once the facility discovered the breach, they were in constant communication with the authorities.

They also had to conduct an internal investigation to get a full accounting of what had been stolen, how deep it went, and how many patients were affected. It took them a couple of days to gather these facts, but at the same time, they knew they had a legal obligation to inform their patients. Because they were unsure of how to go about it, they sought crisis counsel.

We obviously wanted to limit the number of people we needed to alert. There was no point in contacting the entire patient base if only a smaller, finite number had been impacted. But once we knew it was limited in scope, we advised the facility to be as upfront and transparent in their disclosure as possible.

They listened to us and communicated what took place in a very forthright manner. They emphasized their cooperation with law enforcement and promised to stay in touch with the patients and provide ongoing updates. And then they went one step further, offering to assist those affected by actually setting up and paying for identity theft protection for a full year as a sign of goodwill and preventive measure.

Clearly laying out all the facts and next steps in their initial communication went a long way toward putting their patients' minds at ease. The company didn't try to hide any facts; their patient outreach explained everything in detail. There were a handful of calls from people who were very upset, but by and large, the patients were very understanding. They appreciated having received clear communication about what happened.

Mind Your Ps and Fs

A memorable way to think about crisis response done right is what I call the three "f-ups"—Foul Up, 'Fess Up, and Fix Up. The first one is easy enough. We all make mistakes or do things we regret, and some of the errors of our ways are more egregious than others. So yes, the foul up is the trigger.

Then you need to 'fess up. That means acknowledging your wrongdoing and taking responsibility for it. Don't run from it. Address it fully from the start so that it can become old news and be thought of in the past tense.

And lastly, to get any kind of closure and move on from your crisis, you need to fix up. And that involves thinking it through and providing a concrete response, meaning action—not just words. And whatever you say you're going to do, you better make damn sure you deliver on your promise, because people will be watching.

There's another sequence of three to keep in mind: Prevention, Preparation, and Practice. Ideally, all of them need to be set into motion to keep an organization running smoothly in the face of an inevitable crisis.

First, let's consider prevention. Chances are, you'll spend a lot more money on crisis PR consulting and legal bills if you don't take steps on the front end to protect your institution before a crisis erupts. And the best way to do that is to arrange for a crisis communications audit. A comprehensive audit can accurately assess what's most likely to create problems for your organization.

Second is preparation. By knowing where you're vulnerable, you'll be better positioned to put policies and procedures in place that can help keep your organization crisis-free. Preparation means putting together an actionable crisis plan, then making sure there are people in your organization who are fully briefed on it and will know how to execute it if and when the time comes.

The third P is practice, a term that has a double meaning. The first meaning implies putting all your learnings into practice. After all, if you don't adhere to your own best practices, what is the point in creating them anyway? A plan is only effective if you follow it, and therein lies the second meaning, as in practice makes perfect. You need to enact simulations and run crisis drills to know how to react in advance.

Helping people recognize the value of these concepts is an ongoing challenge faced by every crisis communicator. It comes with the territory. There's actually a lot that could be done in advance to help tons of organizations. But too often, the preliminary steps get overlooked. Crisis PR is like insurance. People don't want to pay for it in advance, but when the time comes, they're mighty glad they have it.

CHAPTER 11

IT'S A JUNGLE OUT THERE

As I've stressed throughout this book, most companies are ill-equipped to handle a crisis. After all, it's much easier to turn a blind eye to the warning signs. But given how the odds against you can rapidly escalate, you can't wage a battle for your reputation alone or unprepared and expect to prevail.

If you are not ready and fully prepared to fight, you can get destroyed by enemies—be they known competitors, anonymous haters, or even your own government. There are a whole range of threats out there; there are people preparing at this very moment to take you down.

If you're not willing to stand up for yourself and press the truth, then you can lose everything: your organization and your reputation. Above all, you have to be an advocate for yourself.

When the situation ultimately calls for it, engaging the services of an experienced crisis professional is the way to go. But there are many steps you can take on your own to help prevent a developing crisis from ever reaching that level. What you need are some basic, proven approaches for averting disaster—and a crisis tool kit at the ready to add to the concepts you have already explored in this book.

DIY: Here's Your Crisis Tool Kit

What exactly belongs in your crisis PR tool kit? First and foremost, you need a designated spokesperson—someone equipped to serve as a physical representative of your organization. Whoever it is, this must be someone unafraid to face the cameras, comfortable talking to reporters, poised under pressure, and prepared to put herself or himself on the line for your organization.

In some cases, that could be a top executive; it could be your CEO. Having someone at the executive level confers added authority, but given the limited hours in a day and the demands on their time, sometimes organizations don't want their senior members to serve dual roles. A separate spokesperson may make more sense.

The same holds true at the White House and in Congress. While presidents and members of Congress may like or be equipped to face the press corps themselves, they can't always do so. That's why the spokesperson position exists. That person's job is to speak on behalf of their boss, maintain a dialogue with reporters, and communicate on issues of importance.

Your spokesperson is the public face of the organization and should be battle tested and unflappable in the face of scrutiny. He or she must exhibit certain traits that are critical for success. A qualified spokesman must be able to answer any questions that could arise and field them in a favorable way.

Which brings us to the next necessity. When you designate a spokesperson, this individual has to be media trained and have the ability to synthesize and distill complex information into simple statements.

> Media training is essential preparation for interacting with the public or the press and must be part of your organization's tool kit.

Media training is essential preparation for interacting with the public and the press and must be part of your organization's tool kit.

Media Training: A Deeper Dive

Because it is so important, media training is a core service offering for many crisis management agencies. This systematic training ensures that anyone who completes the process increases his or her confidence and competence when dealing with the media. Look for an effective course taught by a specialized firm with strong crisis PR credentials. Seek out communications training that is comprehensive in nature, providing detailed instructions on how to frame messages and tell stories in a compelling way.

Media training should teach you how to think like reporters and how to anticipate the questions you're most likely to face. Perhaps most importantly, it should prepare you to respond to difficult or challenging inquiries. Be sure that it covers the nuances of speaking in public, such as how to pivot away from potential danger zones into more comfortable topics you would rather discuss. Key is driving positive messaging that frames your organization in the best possible light or conveys your highest priorities.

Once you understand the essentials of effective communications, it's time to build on them so that you fully understand the techniques to help you perform at your best. Of course, just as you have to do with any other skill, you must put theory into practice. And part of that means on-camera simulations with the lights shining on you.

It's the best way to prepare. Training should rehearse simulations of high-pressure media situations, with the camera capturing your every move. There's no room for indecision or missteps. Allow yourself to be recorded as you encounter and respond to high-stress scenarios.

Then, just like a football coach studying film and running the video back and forth to prepare his players, review and critique how you did. Every step of the way pursue instruction, guidance, and advice on how to get better.

Every organization, regardless of size, needs this type of training. Some companies may think it's not necessary for them because they don't regularly hold press conferences or talk to TV reporters. But it's often the people who prepare the least who end up being the ones who need it most.

That's because they haven't acquired or refined these specialized skills. And when that inevitable media situation flares up, they won't know what to do. Public-facing organizations who deal with the media on a regular basis have often developed this discipline on their own. That's the irony. But everyone can always get better.

For companies and organizations, media training has broad implications beyond just press interviews alone. It helps you develop skills which will make you a better communicator, period. So, whether you're talking to investors or employees, strategic partners or vendors, happy customers or disgruntled ones, you'll be able to engage with them more assuredly and effectively. That is the value of media training.

Plan for the Unexpected

I've mentioned this before, but it bears repeating: it is absolutely essential to have a crisis PR plan in place. Your communications tool kit needs to include an actual crisis plan, one that is ready to be deployed at a moment's notice. You need a detailed crisis strategy that will guide you in those initial moments when panic sets in or when pressure reaches a boiling point.

An effective crisis plan actually identifies the areas of the biggest threat and predicts where you're most likely to have issues before they happen. And no crisis plan is complete without a media protocol; another tool kit necessity that should be implemented organization-wide.

A media protocol controls the flow of information so that, externally, people know how they can reach a company representative if they have questions or need information. At the same time, a media protocol is essential internally as well, because people in your organization need to know what is expected of them.

Everyone should receive instruction on how to respond if a reporter calls on the phone and just starts talking to them or if one shows up in person and starts firing away with questions. If a reporter were to walk through the front door with a camera crew, do the receptionist or your other team members know how to react? How to respond? What to do? What to say? If the answer is no, then your organization is at risk.

A crisis plan cannot just sit on a shelf or lie dormant on a network drive or in the cloud. Periodically, you have to conduct an actual crisis run-through. Drilling and practicing are the keys to keeping it effective. It's also important to circulate it with regularity. Another thing you have to do is continuously refresh your plan. After all, the world moves quickly and the media landscape even faster. A crisis plan that you had six months ago is likely not the same one you need today.

Once every year, at a minimum, a crisis plan needs to be taken out, reviewed, examined, and updated. This doesn't have to be a difficult or arduous process, especially if you have done a good job developing it in the first place. If you've been very thorough about crisis PR preparation, then all that's needed are minor tweaks, slight modifications to adapt it to ever-evolving market conditions.

There are some elements that should be in place from square one. You need to have already plotted out a roster of who comprises your crisis response team. You need to determine the key departments that need to be represented, as well as the key executives who must take part. All of this should be laid out in advance.

You also need to have a business continuity plan in place. The COVID-19 pandemic underscored this point perfectly. Every company must ask itself this question: Do we have the infrastructure in place to continue our business operations remotely for an extended time in the event of a crisis?

Then ask: How are you and your associates going to be able to continue doing your jobs? How will you communicate not only with each other but with your key customers? Another crucial item to have is a contact roster that is constantly updated. It should include all members of your crisis response team, as well as the ways to get in touch with them, including phone, email, mobile numbers, and social media handles.

No one knows precisely when the next large-scale crisis is going to hit or what shape it's going to take. Instead of a pandemic, it could be a natural disaster on a regional, national, or global scale. It could be a terrorist incident: a dirty bomb or an attack on the water supply of a municipality. There are a variety of different scenarios that you could imagine, and as recent history has taught us, nothing is too far-fetched. A detailed crisis plan guarantees continuity and the ability to sustain your operation in the face of serious adversity.

Avoiding a Social Media Meltdown

When it comes to your crisis plan, business continuity must be an absolute top priority. You need an ironclad way to lock down all your methods of communication so that they cannot be hijacked. You need a secure way to ensure that your voice mail and your phone system are protected. Adding to that, you must safeguard your email access and make sure that people outside your organization cannot tap into it.

And here is one security measure I cannot stress enough: you need to ensure that key leaders have access to all passwords and login details for every one of your social media accounts.

You would be amazed at the number of times this has been a huge problem at companies, including major global brands. Just picture it: let's say a disgruntled employee on a mission goes on Twitter and starts firing off a stream of incendiary tweets from the official company account. There's no one to rein him in, and he's not holding back; every disparaging comment is affixed to the company name.

> When it comes to your crisis plan, business continuity must be an absolute top priority.

The problem is that all too often, the decision makers and high-ranking executives don't actually maintain control of the accounts. Sometimes it's a generational thing; because they don't really understand social media, they hand over control of social platforms to recent graduates. Then, the company is slow to shut down the accounts or start repairing the damage after an employee goes rogue.

It happens all the time, but please don't let it happen to you. As a business owner or key decision maker, you must maintain command and control over all your social media, for one critical reason: it's an essential way for you to communicate with the world in a time of crisis and one of the first places that people look for information.

Similarly, if you're an enterprise-level business using an intranet, or you have an app that's used to disseminate information company-wide, you must make sure those internal channels are protected too. Just like your external sites, the internal channels must be immediately accessible by the right people so they can be restricted at a moment's notice for reasons of security.

Don't Be Sorry—Be Prepared

As I have said before, a crisis is not the time to acquire on-the-job training. Your tool kit should contain the name and contact details of one or more crisis PR experts—professionals you can count on to be there in your time of need.

Meet them and talk with them ahead of time, even if it's an online video chat. Vet them. Educate them about your organization. And keep in mind that the best time to engage a crisis PR expert is before you find yourself in desperate need of one. That's when they can potentially help you avert a crisis entirely, or at least significantly lessen its impact and empower you to quickly pivot and move past controversy.

Oh, and there is one more thing you should have in your crisis tool kit: this book.

Have it at the ready. Open it up and consult it from time to time. Read through the best practices I have shared and learn from the real-life examples I cite. Then apply them to your own situations. Put

> A crisis is not the time to acquire on-the-job training.

this book on your bookshelf or your desk to serve as a constant reminder that you need to be prepared for any crisis and that there are proven techniques and methods to help you do so successfully.

We are living in a remarkable era when technology, a non-stop news cycle, and conventional and social media can generate an audience of billions that's just one click away. But there's a steep price to be paid. At the risk of being labeled a Cassandra delivering an unheeded message of impending doom, I remind you: serious threats to your reputation are not going away—they're getting worse.

Journalistic ethics are being degraded. Fewer media outlets adhere to a professional editorial process. It is becoming increasingly harder to ensure that you get a fair shake in this world. Bad actors are manipulating Google search algorithms. Anonymous trolls are pushing out content designed to attack you and smear your brand. It is more crucial than ever that you know how to defend yourself and ensure that the truth gets out.

This is precisely why I view crisis management and crisis preparation as an essential part of the business climate and our personal lives today. When you are in an existential fight to protect your livelihood or your good name, you need the right people on your team. You need people who are prepared to charge forward with you, lead you into battle, and be unafraid to take enemy fire to defend what you have worked so hard to achieve.

On behalf of all my colleagues at Red Banyan and crisis managers the world over, I want to congratulate you for taking the time to educate yourself about this crucial topic. Hopefully, you will be able to put much of what you learned in this book to use in your own life. Please remember that if you need help, my colleagues and I are never more than an email, text, tweet, DM, or call away.

If this book helps even a single person or worthy organization avert a crisis or defend their revenue and reputation, then it will have accomplished its goal. I sincerely wish you great success on your own quest to press the truth.

AFTERWORD

One of the reasons I have always loved communications is that the field is in a constant state of flux. While mankind has been telling stories throughout our entire existence, how we actually transmit information is perpetually evolving.

In fact, by the time *Crisis Averted* hits the shelves, new media platforms may have supplanted the old. More timely anecdotes will have emerged.

A book is a labor of love, and it's frustrating to consider that this one will be out of date before it even comes into existence. But I am confident that the concepts I explore will stand the test of time. Plus, the discussion does not need to end here.

The websites www.redbanyan.com and www.evannierman.com are being continuously updated, including with blog posts and analysis exploring the issues of the day. You also can sign up to receive emails containing PR best practices, explore our videos on YouTube, and connect with me directly via Red Banyan's social media, including Facebook, Twitter, LinkedIn, and Instagram.

I welcome the opportunity to exchange ideas and look forward to staying in touch!

—Evan